HOW TO USE CREDIT AND CREDIT CARDS

Revised Edition

Arnold Corrigan
& Phyllis C. Kaufman

D0873072

Longmeadow Press

How to Use Credit and Credit Cards, Revised Edition

Copyright © 1985, 1987 by Arnold Corrigan and
Phyllis C. Kaufman. All rights reserved.

Cover art © 1985 by Longmeadow Press. Design by Adrian Taylor. Production services by William S. Konecky Associates, New York.

Published by Longmeadow Press, 201 High Ridge Road, Stamford, Connecticut 06904. No part of this book may be reproduced or used in any form or by any means, electronic or mechanical, including photocopying, recording, or by any information storage and retrieval system, without permission in writing from the publisher.

No Nonsense Financial Guide is a trademark controlled by Longmeadow Press.

ISBN: 0-681-40245-8

Printed in the United States of America

0 9 8 7 6 5 4 3 2 1

HOW TO USE CREDIT AND CREDIT CARDS

This book will show you:

★ How to get and use credit

★ The best ways to borrow money

★ The different credit cards, what they do, and what they cost

★ What your credit rating is and how to improve it

★ The best way to get an auto loan

★ What your rights are as a credit consumer and how to get a fair deal

THE NO NONSENSE LIBRARY

NO NONSENSE FINANCIAL GUIDES

How to Finance Your Child's College Education
How to Use Credit and Credit Cards, Revised Edition
Understanding Tax-Exempt Bonds, Revised Edition
Understanding Money Market Funds, Revised Edition
Understanding Mutual Funds, Revised Edition
Understanding IRA's
Understanding Treasury Bills and Other U.S. Government Securities, Revised Edition
Understanding Common Stocks, Revised Edition
Understanding the Stock Market, Revised Edition
Understanding Stock Options and Futures Markets, Revised Edition
How to Choose a Discount Stockbroker, Revised Edition
How to Make Personal Financial Planning Work for You
How to Plan and Invest for Your Reitrement
The New Tax Law and What It Means to You

NO NONSENSE REAL ESTATE GUIDES

Understanding Condominiums and Co-ops, Revised Edition
Understanding Buying and Selling a House, Revised Edition
Understanding Mortgages and Home Equity Loans, Revised Edition
Refinancing Your Mortgage, Revised Edition

NO NONSENSE LEGAL GUIDES

Understanding Estate Planning and Wills, Revised Edition
How to Choose a Lawyer

NO NONSENSE CAREER GUIDES

How to Use Your Time Wisely
Managing People—At Home, At Work

NO NONSENSE SUCCESS GUIDES

NO NONSENSE HEALTH GUIDES

NO NONSENSE COOKING GUIDES

NO NONSENSE WINE GUIDES

CONTENTS

To Tillie Corrigan and Ruth Sober, with love

ACKNOWLEDGMENT

The authors wish to express their deep gratitude to Steven L. Osterweis, who helped launch this book to execution; and to Ralph E. Spurgin, who generously shared with us his expert knowledge of the business of credit.

PART I
INTRODUCTION

1 · INTRODUCTION

This is a book about credit.

When you borrow money, you're using credit. When you buy something and pay for it later, you're using credit.

Credit has always played an important part in business. But now *consumer credit*—credit to individuals—also has become a key element in our economy. Individuals in the United States use massive amounts of credit. The government estimates that outstanding consumer credit has risen to well over $500 billion. That's more than $2,000 for each man, woman and child in the United States.

Those numbers don't include more than $1 trillion ($1,000 billion) of home mortgage loans. So when you combine outstanding consumer credit and residential mortgage debt, the total borrowing by individuals turns out to be larger than the much publicized debt of the federal government.

Is all this credit good or bad? As you might suspect, there's no single answer. Credit helps many people live more comfortable, satisfying lives. A minority of people use credit badly and end up in trouble. Also, credit costs money. Some costs are charged to you directly, while others are built into the prices of many of the goods and services we buy.

It's clear that we live in a credit society, yet many of us don't know the answers to such questions as:

- How much can I afford to owe other people?
- What will borrowing cost me in interest and other charges?
- What's the best way to borrow money?
- When can I take a tax deduction for the interest I pay?
- What's the difference between all those plastic cards—store cards, Visa, American Express, etc.?
- How should I finance the purchase of an automobile?
- What is my credit rating and what can I do about it?

These are just a few of the many questions we will answer for you as we describe the mechanics by which other people's money helps you buy everything from housing to hosiery, and helps to pay for doctors, hospitals, schools and colleges as well as food, clothing and transportation.

We'll also discuss the broad range of protective measures that have been passed by the federal and state governments to give you clear rights as a consumer and to ensure that when you use credit, you'll be treated fairly. But to make these rights work for you, you have to know what they are.

We repeat: some people use credit well, others badly. If used well, credit can give you convenience, comfort, and opportunity. This book will give you the guidelines you need to make credit work for you.

2·THE 1986 TAX LAW AND CREDIT

The Tax Reform Act of 1986 changed the income tax rules in ways that are having a broad effect on how people borrow and use credit.

But the changes don't affect everyone. If you itemize deductions on your income tax return, the new rules are almost certainly important to you. On the other hand, if you don't itemize, they may have no direct impact.

Under previous law, any interest you paid on borrowings was tax-deductible, if you itemized. You could, for example, deduct the interest you paid on your automobile loan, your home mortgage, your credit cards, bank loans, education loans, etc.

Now that has changed. Under the Tax Reform Act, different types of interest are treated very differently. Here are the basic rules:

1. Interest paid on a *home mortgage* is still generally tax-deductible. (We'll explain the detailed rules in Chapter 9.)
2. The tax deduction for *consumer interest*—interest on most types of consumer credit, including credit cards, charge accounts, automobile loans, education loans, personal loans, etc.—is being phased out over five years and will disappear in 1991. Here's the timing of the phaseout:

Year	Portion of Interest Deductible
1986	100%
1987	65%
1988	40%
1989	20%
1990	10%
1991 and after	0%

3. *Investment interest*—interest incurred to make or carry investments—remains deductible under the new law, but the deduction is being scaled back so that you won't be allowed to deduct any amounts greater than your investment income.
4. Interest incurred in connection with a *trade or business* remains generally tax-deductible, like most other business expenses.

The New Ball Game

The phaseout of the tax deduction for consumer interest is a major rule change. Obviously, for those who itemize, it makes many kinds of credit more expensive than before.

But the mortgage interest deduction is still available, within certain limits, and American taxpayers are a resourceful group. Even before the ink was dry on the new law, a boom was under way in second mortgages and home equity credit lines (see Chapter 9), as borrowers rushed to take advantage of the mortgage interest deduction as an alternative to other types of borrowing.

Deductions Save You Less

It is important to note that even where deductions are still available, the new tax law has made them worth less than before—by lowering tax rates across the board. Here's a simple example. If you were previously in a 50% federal tax bracket and you paid $1,000 in mortgage interest, deducting the interest on your federal income tax return gave you a tax saving of $500 (50% × $1,000). So the *net cost* to you of the mortgage interest was only $500. But now, if you are in a 28% tax bracket, the same $1,000 deduction will save you only $280 (28% × $1,000). As a result, the *net cost* of your $1,000 interest payment has risen sharply, from $500 to $720.

But Borrowing Continues

So under the Tax Reform Act of 1986, the real cost of borrowing or buying on credit is often higher than before. And, from a tax standpoint, some types of borrowing have become more expensive than others. Given these changes, people can be expected to use credit in somewhat different patterns than they did before. But there is no change in the fact that we live in a credit society, and the intelligent use of credit will continue to be a key to your financial opportunity and well-being.

PART II
CREDIT CARDS AND RETAIL CREDIT

3. RETAIL CREDIT AND CREDIT CARDS

The most common use of credit, or borrowed money, is to help us buy some tangible thing or service. But there are many ways and devices by which the process of retail credit operates, and since each of them has unique characteristics—and, often, different costs—we'll examine these different forms of credit, one by one.

Store Charge Cards and Charge Accounts

Major retail chains and department stores—like Saks Fifth Avenue, J.C. Penney, Macy's and Bloomingdale's, for example—offer their own charge accounts with their own plastic cards. These are *single-purpose* cards, since they can be used for purchases only in the stores of the chain that issues them. Many local stores offer similar arrangements.

30 Days for Free

The credit terms for these single-purpose, merchant-issued cards may vary, but the general structure is usually the same. In effect, if the customer pays all amounts billed within 30 days after the date when the bill was compiled (the "billing date"), then no interest is charged. This is the 30-day "grace period," which in effect gives you 30 days of free credit.

You may not even think of this as a credit transaction, since you're not borrowing money in any obvious way. But it is nevertheless a form of credit, since the store is allowing you a month or more to pay for your purchase. You aren't charged directly for this use of credit, but there is a cost to the store. The cost is simply added to the average price of the merchandise the store sells.

Option Accounts

These accounts also give you the option of stretching out your payments over time. The store statement or bill will usually indicate a minimum required payment which typically will be about one-tenth of the total. This means that the store will let you spread your payments over about a year.

Since you, the customer, have the option of paying your balance either quickly or slowly, this type of account is often referred to as an *option account*.

Revolving Credit

These accounts have another important characteristic. When you open an option account, you sign an agreement with the store. From then on, as long as you pay either the full balance or the required minimum every month, you can continue to buy without ever needing to sign a new agreement or contract with the store. In this way, the account *revolves* through payment and purchase, and hence the other name for these accounts—*revolving credit.*

Monthly Charges

Of course, when you decide to spread your payment over a number of months, or whenever you don't pay the full balance within the 30-day "free" period, *you will be charged interest.* It may be called interest, or a finance charge, or a service charge, but in any case it will be added to your monthly bill.

Under the law, the store or other provider of credit is required to tell you exactly what these charges are and how they are calculated. In Chapter 11, we'll spend some time discussing how the interest charges are figured, and what other service charges you may have to pay.

Some Other Features

The store cards also carry some non-credit attractions. With a "proprietary" credit card, you are on the store's preferred customer list, and you are likely to get advance notices of sales, special promotions, and anything else the store can think of to build your loyalty. Some stores have "bonus point" arrangements which reward you if you buy above a certain amount. With retail competition taking on ever new forms, the stores are likely to do more in this area in the future.

Bank Credit Cards

There are two major bank credit card systems—*Visa* and *MasterCard.* In both systems, the cards are issued by a particular bank or savings institution with which you have an agreement or contract, and to which you will make payments. However, for efficiency and better service, the banks decided some years ago to merge their individual card offerings into either of the worldwide systems—Visa or MasterCard.

Advantages of Bank Credit Cards

As we will see, bank cards have several advantages compared with retail store cards. But almost all banks charge Visa or MasterCard users an annual fee—typically $15 to $20, though the figures vary—and some banks also levy an initial fee when you first obtain your card. (A few banks still issue and maintain the cards without fees—it may be worth shopping around, but you will have to look hard.)

Bank cards have the advantage of being *multi-purpose*, as compared with single-purpose store cards. You can use Visa or MasterCard at a multitude of stores, restaurants, theaters, airlines, hotels, etc. If you think about it, you'll see the great advantage of being able to use a single card at all those establishments, instead of having a separate card for each.

Because banks are in the business of lending money, their cards have certain other advantages. Retail stores generally extend credit to you only as a service and as a way of building customer loyalty—with rare exceptions, they usually don't make a profit on their credit operations. Banks are happy to lend money to you and to see you run up your debit balance (that is, the amount you owe on the account at any given time), as long as you don't exceed your ability to repay. So banks usually set a much lower minimum monthly payment. Where a store may ask you to pay a minimum of 10% of your outstanding balance monthly, a bank may ask for 5% or less, letting you pay off your balance over anywhere from 24 to 36 months—and charging you interest all the time, of course.

And banks are usually glad to *lend* you money—cash, that is—against your credit card. You can usually get a *cash advance* to the extent that you haven't used up your credit line by purchases. So your bank card gives you instant borrowing power.

Credit Line

The size of your credit line may typically be anywhere from $500 to $5,000 or even more, depending on how the bank judges your credit rating when you first apply

10

for a card. Later, if your payment record is good, you can apply to have the ceiling lifted, or the bank will in many cases lift it automatically at intervals based on your record.

Otherwise, bank cards operate much like store-issued single-purpose cards. You're billed monthly, and if the outstanding balance is paid within 25 or 30 days, there's usually no interest charge on your purchases. However, you're almost always charged interest on cash advances from the day you take the advance (as with any other outright loan).

A few banks allow no grace period and also charge interest on *purchases* from the date of purchase. Needless to say, you should avoid any bank with that arrangement unless the bank offers you some offsetting advantage.

Travel and Entertainment Cards

Travel and entertainment (T & E) cards are different from bank credit cards, but the differences are not as great as they used to be. The most widely used T & E card is American Express; others are Diners Club and Carte Blanche.

T & E cards, as the name suggests, were originally usable only at places of entertainment, restaurants, and for airlines and other transportation. Today, however, they're also accepted by many retail stores. Meanwhile, bank cards are now widely accepted for travel and entertainment. So the distinction between bank cards and T & E cards according to where they can be used has largely broken down, and both types of cards are accepted at a very wide variety of places.

T & E Differences

There are, of course, differences. One simple difference is that the American Express card currently costs $45 per year, substantially more than bank cards.

A more fundamental distinction is that the American Express card does *not* give you the automatic option of paying over time. The full amount of the bill is due each month. The card gives you a 30-day free account, but no more. On the other hand, there is no preset limit on how much you can charge to the American Express card each month, as long as you pay your bills promptly and in full.

But in this area too, the banks and American Express are not about to concede any territory to each other, and the lines are rapidly being crossed. American Express now allows extended payments on certain items like airplane tickets. The American Express "gold" card carries a $2,000 line of credit and a $65 annual fee; the company's "platinum" card, offered to its most select customers, costs $250 annually and provides a credit line of $10,000 or more.

The banks have responded with gold MasterCards, gold Visas, and other variations—all offering high credit lines and additional services to individuals with good credit ratings. The annual fee on these premium cards is generally higher than on a basic MasterCard or Visa, but some banks are sweetening the deal by offering lower interest rates on the premium cards.

4. HOW MANY CREDIT CARDS?

How many credit cards should you carry? With the crossing of lines that we've just talked about, a single Visa or MasterCard will be accepted at a surprisingly high percentage of the places where you want to use a card. But there are good reasons for carrying two or three cards, despite the extra annual fees that you'll pay.

Acceptance

First, not all establishments accept all cards. With an assortment, your odds of acceptance are better. There are still many establishments that accept American Express but not the bank cards. At many stores, the reverse is true. Outside the United States, American Express and Visa probably have the widest acceptance. American Express likes to stress that you can get cash advances worldwide by presenting your card at any American Express office.

Computer Frustration

Second, with a few cards you reduce your risk of what we might call Computer Frustration. This is what happens when a merchant checks your credit card standing and either (a) the computer isn't working or (b) it tells the merchant (wrongly) that you're already over your credit limit. In such a case, having another, different card to use can be a blessing.

Increased Credit Limit

Finally (and obviously), the more cards you have, the more total credit you can draw on. Whether this is a danger or an advantage depends on you. If you use your cards carefully, it can be an advantage—especially if your credit line per card is low, as might be the case, for example, if you obtained your cards for the first time only recently.

As you may have gathered from the above, it's quite possible to get separate Visa and/or MasterCards from more than one bank in order to raise your total credit potential. Apart from the extra fees you have to pay, however, this may indicate that you're borrowing more than you should. But there's no law or rule against it, and the banks may not object as long as you pay your minimums on time.

Too Much Credit

However, there may be an unexpected problem in having too many credit lines, even if you use them wisely. When you apply for a new form of credit, the new lender-to-be may pay more attention to the total of your existing credit lines than to what you actually borrow on them.

For example, let's say that you have several bank and retail cards, with credit limits that total $10,000, though your debit balances at present total less than $1,000. If you now apply for an auto loan or a mortgage, the new lender may count your present debt as $10,000 rather than $1,000, since you *could* borrow up to $10,000 on your cards without applying for any additional approval.

Moral: it may be unwise to carry credit lines far above what you actually need. If you find yourself at a disadvantage with a new lender because of the situation we've described, show the lender how you've actually used your cards, and see what you can work out.

5·RETAIL CREDIT— INSTALLMENT ACCOUNTS AND OTHER VARIATIONS

Typically, both single-purpose and multi-purpose charge cards have limits on the total amount of credit that the issuer will extend to the customer or card-holder. For most of us, these limits give us enough credit to buy clothing, travel, entertainment, dining, etc. But credit limits are usually not high enough to let us finance the purchase of a major item—an automobile or a roomful of furniture, for example.

For buying more expensive items, different kinds of credit arrangements come into play. Many large stores have an "easy payment" plan, under one name or another, whereby eligible customers can buy larger items on credit and pay them off over 24 months or more. These are separate from the store's regular charge accounts; in some ways they resemble a large-size revolving account, but usually a specific monthly payment is set so that the customer will pay for the purchase completely over a certain number of months.

Other establishments, such as furniture stores, may use *conditional sales contracts*, which is what we generally think of as "buying on the installment plan." A conditional sales contract is *not* an open or revolving account. It is arranged and contracted for in connection with a specific transaction, and it usually permits the merchant to repossess the merchandise if the customer doesn't meet the monthly payments.

Payment Terms

A conditional sales contract on a smaller item might call for payments stretching out over only a year, but on larger items the payment period may be two years, or even more in special cases. (In autos, as we will see in the next chapter, the five-year loan has now entered the scene.)

Under both the store plans and the installment plan purchases, you repay the loan in level payments—identical monthly amounts over the repayment period. By contrast, if you are paying down a debit balance on a credit card, the required minimum payment will drop each month as the size of your balance is reduced.

For example, if you buy a $1,000 set of furniture on installment and contract to pay for it over two years (24 months) at an 18% interest rate, your repayment schedule might look like this:

A)	Monthly payment	$ 49.92
B)	Total payments (A × 24)	1,198.08
C)	Total interest paid (B less $1,000)	198.08

The total interest charge is sizeable, yet you might have assumed it would be even higher. Borrowing $1,000 for one year at 18% should cost $180, by simple arithmetic, and for two years it should cost $360, not $198. But this ignores the fact that you have been paying your balance down month-by-month, and that the interest is calculated each month based only on the principal balance that you still owe.

What this means is that while your *payments* are level, the breakdown between principal and interest changes. Early in the repayment period, a bigger part of each payment goes for interest; near the end of the period, when the loan balance is reduced, the interest charges are small. Each month, what is left over after paying interest goes to reduce the principal of the loan, with the payments calculated so that the principal will be paid off exactly at the end of the repayment period.

Advantages and Disadvantages

A conditional sales contract is often offered to buyers who might not qualify for a charge account or credit card. Why? Because the seller usually has the right to *repossess* the merchandise if the buyer doesn't keep up with the monthly payments. So these loans are *secured* loans, with the merchandise itself being the security.

As with many things in life, this is part good, part bad. The arrangement makes credit available to many people who otherwise couldn't get it. But having merchandise repossessed can be an extremely unpleasant experience, and it does happen. (For a discussion of how much debt you can reasonably carry, see Chapter 18.)

Merchants often use long-term credit arrangements as a form of price competition—in effect, a price concession under a different name. If this takes the form of a lower interest rate—or, occasionally, an interest-free period at the beginning of the loan—it can be a real advantage to the buyer. But if the merchant is merely letting you have lower monthly payments by stretching your loan out over a longer period, he or she is probably not doing you a favor.

Resisting Temptation

Unfortunately, many consumers buy big-ticket items wherever the monthly payment is lowest. Of course, the payments can always be made lower by lengthening the repayment period.

If you're buying something you really need and that will last many years—for example, an auto—a long repayment period may make sense and may even be necessary. But too often, stretched-out terms lure people into buying higher-priced goods that don't really fit into their budgets. Frequently the buyer ends up unable to meet the payments—or with no borrowing power left when a real necessity or emergency comes along.

PART III
OTHER FORMS OF BORROWING

6·AUTO FINANCING

The financing of automobile purchases is a form of installment contract. Next to financing a home, an auto purchase is likely to be the largest debt transaction the average consumer ever makes.

Surveying the Choices

As anyone knows who reads the newspaper or watches television, competition on credit terms is an important part of auto sales promotion. And since auto financing has become highly profitable, there is also considerable competition for your credit business among the manufacturer's own finance company, independent auto finance companies, and regular banks.

Dealer Financing

What are your choices? Car buyers expect to be able to get financing from their dealer if they need it, and your auto dealer will almost certainly have a "dealer floor plan" to offer.

Ordinarily, the dealer plan will *not* be your best alternative. The plan usually has a profit in it both for the dealer and for the finance company or bank with which the dealer cooperates. This double profit is built into your cost.

However, there are special times when the dealer may be your best bet for financing. At intervals, the major auto companies run promotions where their captive finance companies (GMAC, etc.) arrange for the dealer to offer low, subsidized interest rates for a limited period, as a special sales inducement. If you're offered one of these special deals at 2% or 3% below the going rate—and if it isn't offset by the dealer's adding a few hundred dollars to the price of the car—you have a good deal.

Bank Financing

Your best bet may be to shop around among the local banks. Banks like car loans—the loans are relatively large and easy to service, and it's always possible to repossess the car if the buyer doesn't meet his or her payments.

What Rate Will You Pay?

Interest rates on auto loans are substantially lower than rates on the types of consumer credit we've discussed in previous chapters. Autos are big-ticket items, so that the administrative costs to the bank or other lender are small relative to the size of the loan. In early 1987, auto loans were widely available at 9½% to 10%, compared with the 16% to 21% rates generally being charged on charge accounts and credit cards.

If you are in a high income bracket and have an "executive-type" line of credit with your bank, compare the interest rate on your credit line with the available rates on car loans. A car loan will probably be cheaper, but it's worth making the comparison.

The Home Equity Alternative

Under the Tax Reform Act of 1986, the interest you pay when you borrow against your home is tax-deductible, within certain limits, while the interest on other types of borrowing is not. (See Chapter 2.) So in some cases it may make sense to finance a car by borrowing against your home. Calculate your tax savings carefully, and remember the general risks of home equity borrowing. (See Chapter 9.) The costs of setting up a home equity credit line can be sizable, and it may not be worth incurring those costs only for a car purchase. But if you already have a home equity credit line at a bank or stockbroker, this might be the cheapest way to finance your new car.

The Leasing Alternative

You may want to consider *leasing* a car rather than buying. Often the monthly lease payments are lower than loan payments would be on the same car—but at the end of the lease period, you don't own the car unless you make an additional lump payment. Under the old tax law, when the interest you paid on an auto loan was fully deductible, the tax deduction counted as one reason to buy rather than lease; now that advantage is being phased out.

Some lenders are now offering car loans with lower monthly payments, to compete with a lease, but with a lump-sum or "balloon" payment at the end. This may suit the buyer who expects to sell the car at the end of the loan period, and who will be able to meet the balloon payment out of the proceeds of sale; otherwise, it's a dangerous arrangement unless you're absolutely sure that you'll have some other means of meeting the balloon payment.

How Long a Loan?

As pointed out above, some lenders will now let you reduce your monthly auto loan payments by stretching them out over five years (60 months) instead of the more usual four years (48 months). Should you do it?

There's no simple answer. If you are buying an expensive, well-built car which you expect to own for six or seven years, it may be reasonable to take a five-year loan. But if you're using the five-year loan to buy a more expensive car than you normally would consider, think twice. Remember that it can be a great advantage to have the loan paid off before the car is old enough to need expensive major repairs.

(For more information on the pitfalls of auto financing, see Chapter 12.)

7·BORROWING CASH

All the forms of credit we've discussed so far have been related mainly to transactions for the purchase of specific goods or services. But you can also borrow cash directly in order to get past an emergency, or to cover purchases, or for any one of a number of good reasons.

Nowadays, getting a "consumer loan" is often an easy matter. But it was not always so. At one time, the only source of credit for many people was the "loan shark" who charged brutally high interest rates. And even when more respectable institutions made such personal loans, then often called "small loans," there was often abuse and inordinately high rates. The consumer finance companies that specialized in small loans generally had mixed reputations.

Government regulations, both state and federal, have been important in bringing protection to the consumer in this field. But perhaps most important has been the increased availability of cash from new, legitimate sources.

Getting Cash from Banks

The consumer loan field has been changing rapidly in recent years. You can easily obtain moderate cash advances on your bank credit card. Most commercial banks with retail branches now make various types of consumer loans. Savings banks and savings and loan associations, which once were limited primarily to mortgage lending, have begun to make consumer loans. Competition in the field is active. As a result, some of the old "small loan" companies have now largely abandoned the field and have turned to making second mortgage or "home equity" loans. (See Chapter 9.)

Shop Around

As always, when there's competition, it pays to shop around. See what cash advances are available on your credit cards, and what interest rates are being charged. Try the various banks and savings institutions in your area and ask their terms.

Although each bank usually has a fixed schedule of terms and interest rates, they are sometimes subject to negotiation—especially at your own bank, if you have a good record. It can't hurt to try.

Overdraft Accounts

Many banks have introduced *overdraft* arrangements of one sort or another. An overdraft lets you write checks for more dollars than you have in your checking account, with the bank lending you the excess. These accounts go under such names as "privilege checking," etc. As with a cash advance on a credit card, these arrangements have the advantage of letting you borrow just what you need and for as long as you need; repayments are likely to be required at about the same rate as with a credit card advance.

Credit Line

Even if your bank offers no formal overdraft arrangement, try asking for a prearranged credit line. If your credit rating is good, you may get it. What you want is an *unsecured* credit line, which costs nothing to arrange. Nowadays, the bank is likely to suggest a *home equity* credit line (see Chapter 9), which is much more complicated and expensive to set up. As we'll see, the home equity credit line can be an important resource for you, but it should be avoided unless you contemplate major borrowing over a long period of time.

Borrowing from Credit Unions

The credit union is a special kind of institution designed to make credit available at low cost to the small individual borrower.

Federal credit unions were authorized by a 1934 statute as a sort of cooperative credit organization, and they are regulated by the federal government. Members are depositors, and only members can be borrowers. Deposits in federally chartered credit unions are insured up to $100,000 by the U.S. government, and borrowers benefit because the regulations that govern credit unions place a ceiling on the interest rate that they can charge on loans—a ceiling that is close to the lowest commercial rates in the market at the time.

So, if you have access to a federal credit union through your job or through some organization to which you belong, you will probably do well to join and become a depositor. This will make you eligible for the credit union's low-cost loans. Then, when you need to borrow, you're likely to find that the credit union will give you a better deal than anyplace else in town.

8·HOME FINANCING— GETTING A MORTGAGE

The purchase of a home is usually the largest credit transaction a person ever makes. Because a home is likely to cost more than a family's annual income— often as much as three or even four times annual income—credit is essential, whether you're buying a single-family home, condominium or co-op.

In buying a house or condo, you take out a mortgage loan, meaning that you *mortgage* or *pledge* your home as security for the loan. Because the lender has this security, and because of the large size of the loan, interest rates on mortgage loans are much lower than those on retail consumer credit, and much closer to the market interest rates that prevail on business borrowings.

But because of the size and length of a mortgage loan, all the terms of the loan, including the interest rate, are critical for a home buyer. Seemingly small variations can greatly raise or lower the costs you incur over the life of the loan, which may be as long as 30 years.

The Mortgage Tax Break

As we pointed out in Chapter 2, the Tax Reform Act of 1986 has given mortgages a privileged position compared with other types of borrowing. While the tax deduction on most types of "consumer interest" is being phased out, interest paid on a home mortgage is still generally deductible. We'll say more about the specific tax rules in Chapter 9.

How a Mortgage Loan Works

The many things you need to know about mortgages can fill a separate book, and we recommend to you the No Nonsense Real Estate Guides, *Understanding Mort-*

26

gages and *Refinancing Your Mortgage.* Here we'll mention only a few key facts to keep in mind.

In a traditional "fixed-rate" mortgage, there is a fixed interest rate and fixed monthly payments over the life of the loan. In a "variable-rate" mortgage, the rate and the size of the payments can vary.

With either type, a large part of your monthly payment in the early years represents interest on the loan, which will generally be tax-deductible for federal income tax purposes. As the principal amount of the loan is gradually paid down, less and less of each payment represents interest (since the monthly interest is calculated on the actual remaining balance of the loan), and more and more of each payment represents repayment of principal.

Variable-Rate Mortgages

Because of the very wide swings in interest rates in recent years, lenders have become less willing to commit their funds for 20 or 30 years at a single prearranged interest rate, and, when interest rates are running high, borrowers are likely to have similar feelings. So there has come into existence the *variable-rate mortgage*, often called an *adjustable-rate mortgage* or *ARM*.

In an ARM, the interest rate is adjusted periodically according to some accepted index of interest rates, such as the current rate on U.S. Treasury bills or some other class of U.S. government securities. Usually the mortgage agreement sets limits on how much the interest rate can vary at each adjustment, and how much it can vary over the entire life of the loan.

The periodic adjustments usually mean a change in the amount of your monthly payment, though in a certain type of ARM a change is made instead in the *number* of monthly payments that will be required to pay off the loan.

When you take out an ARM you are, in a sense, speculating on the future course of interest rates. If interest rates decline, you'll benefit by paying less over the life of the mortgage. If interest rates rise, you'll pay more. But because you've taken out an ARM, which reduces the lender's long-term risk, the lender has, in almost all cases, probably given you a lower initial interest rate than you would have been given on a fixed-rate mortgage.

Shop, Shop, Shop

As you can see, it is vital to study the terms of a mortgage loan carefully, and to shop for the best available deal. Over 20 or 30 years, a small difference in initial terms can add up to a major difference in dollars.

9·HOME EQUITY LOANS

If you already own a home, it is likely to be by far your biggest potential source of credit. And, as we have seen, the new tax law generally lets you deduct interest payments when you borrow against your home, while the deduction on many other types of interest is being phased out.

There are several ways you can borrow against your home:

1. If you have no mortgage on your home, you can take out a mortgage.
2. You can *refinance* your mortgage—that is, take out a new mortgage to replace the old. If the new mortgage is for a larger amount than the remaining balance on the old mortgage, the extra cash is yours to use any way you want. (See the No Nonsense Real Estate Guide, *Refinancing Your Mortgage*.)
3. You can keep your old mortgage and arrange for a *second mortgage* to provide additional cash.
4. You can keep your old mortgage and arrange for a *home equity loan* or *home equity credit line*, which is a newer, more flexible alternative to the traditional second mortgage.

All these borrowing arrangements are based on your *equity* in your home, which is the market value of your home, minus whatever mortgage or other debts you already owe on it.

How the Tax Rules Work

If you are considering borrowing on your home in order to benefit from the mortgage interest deduction, or for any other reason, you need to know how the new tax rules work. As we've said, interest on a home mortgage is still generally deductible. But there are limits.

First, the deduction for "qualified housing interest" under the 1986 law *is limited to interest on debt taken against a taxpayer's principal residence or second residence only.*

Second, with the exceptions noted below, *the debt on which interest is deductible may not exceed the cost basis of the property*—the original purchase price plus the cost of any improvements. (Obviously, you must keep careful track of the amount spent on improvements.)

1. Exception #1: *If you refinanced your mortgage or took out a new mortgage before August 17, 1986,* the mortgage can be up to the fair market value of the property, and the interest will still be fully deductible, even if the fair market value exceeds the cost basis.
2. Exception #2: The debt can exceed your cost basis to the extent it is incurred for *educational or medical expenses,* and the interest will still be deductible.

Note that the debt must be on a *residence.* This means that if you own land on which you hope someday to build a vacation home, any interest you pay on a loan against that land will not be deductible as long as no residence has yet been built on the land.

Unlocking Your Home Equity

What do the new rules mean in practical terms to you, as a homeowner? If your mortgage was for a low percentage of cost in the first place, or if it has been paid down to an amount below your cost basis, you can borrow an additional amount up to the cost basis and still deduct the interest for tax purposes.

However, the tax deduction isn't the only point to consider. The fair market value of your home may have risen far above your original cost, and you may be able to borrow up to about 80 percent of this fair market value. Under the new rules, the interest on the amount borrowed above the cost basis will not be tax-deductible; but this method of borrowing will generally give you an interest rate considerably lower than other consumer interest rates (and note the educational-medical exception).

As noted above, one way of tapping the extra equity in your home is by refinancing your existing mortgage. For the pros and cons of this approach, see the No Nonsense Real Estate Guide, *Refinancing Your Mortgage.*

If your old mortgage is at a favorable rate, you should then consider the other ways of borrowing additional amounts on your home. As we pointed out above, you can take out a second mortgage, or a home equity credit line.

Second Mortgages

A second mortgage is an additional mortgage loan that you take out based on the equity you own in your home. The second mortgage lender has a lien on your home, just as the first mortgage lender, but the second is "junior" to the first; in case of foreclosure, the second mortgage lender must wait until the primary lender is paid off in full before he or she can collect. To arrange a second mortgage, you may have to go through many of the same procedures and costs you originally incurred in getting your first mortgage—credit check, appraisal, title search, attorneys' costs, etc. If the new mortgage is with the same lender as the old, you may be able to short-cut some of this, but otherwise it could cost you $2,000 or more to go through this process. Obviously, it's not a step to be taken lightly.

Interest rates on second mortgages generally are higher than on first mortgages, because of the junior position the second lender must assume. But a second mortgage may make sense if you need to borrow a substantial amount of cash for a substantial period of time. Most second mortgages are fixed-rate loans, but some lenders also offer variable-rate arrangements.

Home Equity Loans

Another way of borrowing on your home equity is the home equity loan, which is really a newer and more flexible form of second mortgage.

Home equity loans are the latest and "hottest" way of unlocking the extra credit power in your house. Banks, savings and loans, brokerage firms, mortgage bankers, and finance companies have all jumped on this new bandwagon.

Though the advertisements don't stress the fact, setting up this sort of credit arrangement usually costs money, just as with a second mortgage. In most cases, the lender puts you through a full mortgage check (appraisal, credit check, etc.); and recording, title insurance, points, and other fees may have to be paid. However, when the competition for home equity loans is keen, lenders may waive all or some of these charges, so it pays to compare several loan sources.

Varieties of Home Equity Loans

There are two major types of home equity loans. The first is similar to a second mortgage in that a lump sum is borrowed and paid back over a specified period of time, with either a fixed or a floating interest rate. We suggest that a fixed-rate arrangement is preferable if the interest rate is reasonable. The floating rate carries the same risk for the borrower as with an adjustable-rate mortgage: it can be troublesome if interest rates rise over the course of repayment.

The second type is a revolving charge, usually called a home equity line of credit. The line is set up with a certain maximum amount of money available. You can tap into the line whenever you wish, either all at once, or in smaller doses. You pay interest only on the actual amount borrowed, but you pay the charges for setting up the line whether or not you use it. There may or may not be a fixed repayment schedule—some lenders permit you to keep a debt balance indefinitely as long as you maintain regular interest payments. More typical is a repayment schedule of ten years (120 months). Interest rates can either be fixed or floating; again, we stress that a fixed rate is preferable, though many of these arrangements are available only with a floating rate.

How Much Can You Borrow?

The amount you can borrow on a second mortgage or a home equity loan is best shown by an example. Let's say that your house is appraised at $120,000, and the lender's practice is to lend up to 80 percent of the appraised value. In your case, that amounts to $96,000. But you still owe a balance of $60,000 on your first mortgage. The lender subtracts $60,000 from $96,000 and arrives at $36,000, which is the net amount available for you to borrow. (Of course, if $96,000 is greater than your cost basis, not all the interest you pay will be tax-deductible.)

Some Pitfalls

Home equity loans can be useful. But there are a few important warnings. First, make sure you understand all the rules and costs. What will you be charged for the initial appraisal and the other costs of setting up the loan or credit line? Will you have to repeat the whole procedure at the end of five years, or whenever the initial period expires? How will the interest rate be figured? On what schedule will repayments be due? Can the repayments be spread over a sufficiently long period?

Second, remember that if you have a floating interest rate—as is true with most equity lines of credit—the interest rate you pay will adjust periodically according to some index, such as the bank's prime loan rate. And ordinarily *there is no cap* on the interest rate you may have to pay. If interest rates generally rise, you may be stuck with higher interest rates whether you can afford them or not. And if you want to repay your loan early, be aware that some equity lines with a fixed repayment schedule carry a prepayment penalty.

Finally, don't enter into a home equity loan without remembering that *the lender has a lien on your house*. This isn't just a personal loan—it's the equivalent of a mortgage. So even if the interest rate will be lower than on a personal loan, and even if you are tempted by the tax deduction, make sure that you can repay what you borrow before you put your house at risk.

10·SOME OTHER WAYS OF BORROWING

In Chapter 7, we discussed some of the simpler ways of borrowing cash, as on a bank credit card advance. But if you need to borrow any substantial amount of cash, the use of a bank credit card advance is an expensive way to proceed. Banks are happy with this type of business—an advance of from $500 to $5,000 or even more, at an APR of perhaps 18% to 20%, is a highly profitable item.

Many banks push offerings of "executive credit" lines to higher-income individuals, sometimes at even higher rates than the regular credit card charges. And a standard unsecured small loan from a bank is usually also a high-cost item.

So if you have a legitimate need to borrow, you should look for other ways to do it. What if you don't own a home, or if you don't wish to borrow on your home equity? Depending on your situation, we'll look at some of the other possibilities that may be open to you.

Borrowing on Your Life Insurance

If you carry *permanent* or *whole life* insurance in which there is a buildup of *cash value* or *surrender value*, your policy almost certainly has a provision for borrowing against the cash value, often to as much as 95% of this value, and without time limit. If the policy is an old one, the interest rate on such a policy loan may be between 5% and 10%—the older the policy, the lower the rate is likely to be. If you have such a policy, it may be the cheapest source of credit you can find. (But note that the interest you pay will generally *not* be tax-deductible.)

If you carry only *term* life insurance, in which no cash value is built up, this option of course won't apply to you. That doesn't mean you've made a mistake—from many points of view, term life is a better buy than permanent life, but it does *not* include a savings component, and so there's nothing to borrow on.

If you do have permanent life, the borrowing procedure should be relatively simple. But remember that any amount you borrow reduces your insurance coverage. Say that you have a $25,000 whole life policy with a cash value of $6,000, and you borrow $4,000 against the cash value. If you die while the loan is outstanding, your beneficiary will receive only $21,000 (the face value of $25,000, less the $4,000 loan). If you owe any accrued interest on the loan, that will be deducted too. So use this option carefully.

Borrowing from Your Retirement Plan

Your company pension or profit-sharing plan may contain provisions allowing you to borrow against your interest in the plan. Ask about it, since this type of loan can be a bargain if you need credit. The interest rate will vary from plan to plan, but often it is set on some basis that keeps rates not too far above the market rates currently charged on business borrowings.

We repeat that the rules will depend on the individual plan. But under the law, such loans can't be for more than the *lesser* of (a) one-half of your vested dollar interest in the plan or (b) $50,000. However, if the loan is for less than $10,000, limit (a) doesn't apply.

The *term* of the loan is limited by law to five years, unless the loan is for purchase of a principal residence.

As with loans against life insurance, remember that a loan against your retirement plan puts a dent in one of the most important assets you have. If you retire or die while the loan is outstanding, the amount of the benefit to you or your beneficiary will be reduced by the amount of the loan. And if you fail to repay the loan within the legally required period, the amount that you fail to repay will be treated for income tax purposes as a taxable distribution to you.

Borrowing against Stocks and Bonds

If you own securities, they can be a very favorable source of credit. Brokers are permitted to lend on *margin* against stocks and bonds, and banks also can lend against securities as collateral. Most actively traded issues are eligible for margin loans; in recent years, the rules have let you borrow up to 50% of market value on stocks and convertible bonds, and more on other types of bonds.

Do some shopping to make sure that you are using a broker who charges low interest rates. Some brokers may charge their margin customers as little as 1/2 of 1% above the *broker's call loan rate,* which is the rate at which the broker is borrowing money from the banks. But some brokers may take a much wider spread. Make sure you know what you will be charged, and whether there will be any other account charges that will increase your costs.

Just because you are borrowing against stocks and bonds doesn't mean that the interest you pay will necessarily be tax-deductible. That depends on the *purpose* of the borrowing. If you are borrowing to buy or carry securities or other investments, then the interest you pay is investment interest, deductible up to the limit of your net investment income. This applies, for example, when you buy a stock on margin, putting up 50% of the cost and borrowing the other 50% from your broker. But if you borrow against your securities to buy a boat or a car, the interest becomes consumer interest, subject to the usual consumer interest rules.

Don't lose sight of the fact that you are pledging your securities in order to incur debt, no matter how favorable the terms may be. If the market value of your securities should drop sharply, the broker will ask you to put up more cash or collateral; eventually, if you can't meet the requirements, the broker has the right to sell the securities at whatever the current market value may be and take out the amount owed. Margin borrowing, like other forms of debt, is not for the careless.

Some banks are now offering *investment accounts* under various names, which include a provision for margin borrowing. These accounts may include such features as high money market interest rates for your cash; withdrawal of cash by check or debit card (the type of card used at automatic teller machines); buying and selling of stocks, bonds, and other investment items, usually on a discount brokerage basis; and borrowing against your securities. The arrangement may be a convenient one, but make sure you know the borrowing costs and other charges before you begin. The law requires that you be told how interest charges will be figured.

PART IV
HOW MUCH CREDIT COSTS

11 · UNDERSTANDING CREDIT CHARGES

As we've seen in the preceding chapters, credit is one of the most important things that the American consumer buys, and the *cost* of credit is important to almost everyone's budget.

Some Arithmetic

It may be useful to explain some fundamentals. The cost of credit is primarily the *interest* you pay on money you borrow. And we've found that a surprising number of people aren't clear about how to calculate interest charges.

Calculating Percent

Interest is expressed as a *percent*. Most pocket calculators have a percent (%) key and instructions on how to use it. If not, since percentages represent *hundredths*, move the decimal point two places to the left to translate percentages into decimals:

12½%	=	12.5%	=	.125
15¾%	=	15.75%	=	.1575

If you don't know the decimal equivalent of a fraction, find it by dividing on the calculator. For example, ⅞ = .875 (7 divided by 8), so 16⅞% = .16875.

Calculating the Time Period

Unless otherwise specified, the interest rate always represents an *annual* rate. So to find the dollars you actually pay on a credit transaction, you have to put the number of years into the calculation. For example, if you borrow $5,000 for two years, paying interest at 9½% annually, with the whole sum repaid at the end of the two years, your total interest payments are $5,000 × .095 × 2 = $950.

If you're dealing with a time period that's not an even number of years, you must translate it into years. If the period is expressed in months, simply divide by 12 to convert to years. For example, if the period in the above example were 33 months instead of two years, the arithmetic would be $5,000 × .095 × 33/12 = $1306.25. If the period were expressed as four years and three months, you would either know or calculate that three months is .25 years (since 3/12 = .25), and the interest calculation would then be $5,000 × .095 × 4.25 = $2018.75.

Compounding

You also need to be clear about how *compounding* works. The simplest illustration of compounding is not when you use credit, but when you put money in a bank savings account. Almost everyone has seen the interest rate tables posted by banks to show what their different accounts are paying at the moment. For each account, two figures are posted—the interest rate, and the *effective yield* or just plain *yield*. The reason for the "effective yield," (or just plain "yield") figure is that because of compounding, your money earns more interest in a year than is shown by the interest rate alone.

You might assume that at 8%, a $1,000 deposit will earn $80 for the year ($1,000 × .08), but actually it will do better. If interest is compounded quarterly, at the end of the first quarter, $20 will be added to your account ($1,000 × .08/4). Then, in the second quarter, you will be earning interest not on $1,000, but on $1,020. At the end of the second and third quarters this process will be repeated. At the end of the year, your account will total not $1,080, but $1,082.43.

If interest were compounded *daily*, each day's interest would be added to the account *that day*, without waiting for the end of the quarter, and the buildup would go even a little faster.

In these examples, of course, you're not a borrower but a saver (in effect a lender, lending your money to the bank). When you're a *borrower*, compounding is likely to work against you, adding to your interest costs. For example, in some charge accounts and credit card accounts, if you miss a payment, the unpaid interest is allowed to compound, while in others it is not. Compounding means that in the next period, you're charged interest on the unpaid interest. It may not make a big difference in dollars, but it's worth noting.

Interest Rate vs. Interest Charges

Finally, and perhaps most important, you have to be clear about the distinction between the interest *rate* you pay and the total interest *charges*. For example, let's say you borrow $1,000 for a year at 12% interest. At the end of the year you pay back the $1,000 plus $120 in interest. Simple enough.

But what if you buy a set of furniture for $1,000 and the lender tells you that the finance charge is $117.32 (which looks like a little less than 12%) and that you'll pay back the total of $1,117.32 in twelve monthly installments of $93.11 each? Although the total dollars you pay back are slightly less than in the previous example, the situation is quite different.

Since you're making payments throughout the year, you only have the use of the full $1,000 at the beginning of the year, and the actual size of your loan diminishes steadily as the year goes on. The *average* size of your loan during the year is only a little more than half the starting $1,000. If the total finance charge of $117.32 is related to this *average* loan size, it turns out that the real interest rate you are paying—what is termed the *annual percentage rate* —is not just under 12%, but 21%.

But while 21% may sound forbidding, don't let it frighten you. Take a moment to look at it in reverse. Let's say you're negotiating for that $1,000 set of furniture and the merchant tells you, as the law requires, that you will pay an annual percentage rate of 21%. If you're making regular monthly payments, you will *not* be paying $210 in interest. Actually, you'll pay the same $93.11 per month and your total interest payments will be the same $117.32. This may seem a very reasonable price to pay for having the furniture now rather than saving up for a year, especially if you think that the price a year from now will be higher.

Help from Uncle Sam

Calculating true interest rates is often difficult. But fortunately, as a user of credit you benefit from a remarkably complete set of federal laws that give you more protection, as a consumer of credit, than exists in almost any other consumer area.

These laws don't regulate the amount of interest or the interest rate that you can be charged. But they do force lenders to disclose all the information you need to shop for credit intelligently, and they do protect you against discrimination in lending and unfair practices.

Truth in Lending Act

The Truth in Lending Act of 1968 has been called a landmark piece of legislation. It not only requires lenders to make full disclosure of the cost of borrowing, but also requires them to state the cost in a standardized form that makes it easy for you to compare one charge with another and know just what your costs will be.

This is how Congress set forth the purpose of the Act:

> *The informed use of credit results from an awareness of the cost thereof by consumers. It is the purpose of this title to assure a meaningful disclosure of credit terms so that the consumer will be able to compare more readily the various credit terms available to him and avoid the uninformed use of credit, and to protect the consumer against inaccurate and unfair credit billing and credit card practices.*

The Act distinguishes, as we did in Chapter 3, between open-end or revolving credit, and closed-end credit, which includes all other types.

Under the Act, the lender or seller in all instances is required to give the consumer basic information *before* the first credit transaction. In the case of *open-end* or revolving credit, the information that must be given includes:

1. The length of the "free period"—the time during which the consumer can pay the outstanding balance without incurring any finance charge.
2. The interest rate that will be charged on your balance, expressed as an *annual percentage rate* or APR.
3. Exactly how the lender will calculate the balance on which this interest rate is charged.
4. Any membership fee, transaction fees, or other fees or charges that may be imposed.

In the case of *closed-end* credit, such as an installment loan, the lender or seller must give you the following information:

1. The amount of the down payment.
2. The *amount financed*, which is the total amount you are borrowing.
3. The repayment schedule and, except in the case of housing loans, the sum of all the payments.
4. The total *finance charge*, which is the total dollar amount you will pay for the credit—including not only the interest costs, but possibly such other charges as service charges, insurance premiums, etc. (In the case of a mortgage, there are likely to be special fees for an appraisal, etc.)
5. The total finance charge expressed as an *annual percentage rate* or APR.

The Truth in Lending Act also applies to advertising. There's no restriction on a merchant or lender's making general statements in advertising, such as "easy financing terms" or "no down payment." But if the ad offers any specific figures—even so simple a statement as "30 months to pay"—then the law requires that the ad disclose several of the key pieces of information which we have just discussed, including in particular the APR.

Read the Fine Print

With all this information available, why do consumers make mistakes when taking on credit transactions? You guessed it—many consumers don't bother to read the fine print. Get in the habit of knowing your credit terms. Once you understand the words and know what the seller or lender is required to tell you, you can have the profit and pleasure of being an informed consumer instead of an easy target. And especially on large transactions, you may save youself considerable money.

Some credit card solicitations offer you a card without telling you the cost of the card or the interest rate you will be charged on your balance. You receive this information only when you receive the card.

The card issuer can get away with this because, technically, you are still getting the information *before the first credit transaction*. It's legal, but it's certainly not what the Truth in Lending Act had in mind. Of course, you can send the card back and hope not to be dunned for the fee. But we would certainly avoid ordering a credit card on those terms.

Comparison Shop

When comparison shopping, make a point of understanding clearly the different credit terms you are offered. This doesn't mean that you should always pick the credit with the lowest APR. If you're very short of cash, you might decide to pay a higher APR in order to be permitted a lower down payment or a longer repayment period. Or you might be offered the same merchandise from two different sellers, and at one of them a lower selling price for the merchandise might more than offset a higher APR on the credit arrangement.

Often there are many variables to juggle. But if you know your credit costs clearly, the odds are good that you will be on your way to an intelligent decision.

12·HOW MUCH WILL CREDIT COST?

How much will you really pay for credit? Certain types of consumer credit are relatively expensive compared with the rates on business and government borrowings. But how much you pay depends very much on the type of credit you select.

On a large loan, such as a home mortgage, the interest rate set by a lender depends primarily on the general level of interest rates in the economy at a given time. The lender's costs in arranging the loan and monitoring repayments may be substantial, but they are not large in relation to the size of the loan and the total interest payments over the life of the loan.

In revolving credit accounts and bank credit card accounts, the situation is different. Here the administrative costs are large in relation to the interest charges. Even if interest rates in the economy fall generally to a low level, rates on these accounts are likely to stay high so that lenders can cover their costs of operation.

Let's take the level of rates in early 1987 as an example. In early 1987, after a few years of declining interest rates, the "prime rate" charged by banks to their borrowers stood at 7½%. The average mortgage rate on new homes, which had risen above 15% in the early 1980s, was down in the 9½–10% range. Some auto loan rates with APRs below 8% were being advertised, but these appeared to be subsidized rates for sales promotion purposes; the real rate on auto loans appeared also to be in the 9½–10% range.

At the same time, APRs on store credit accounts and bank credit cards remained mainly in the 16–21%

area where they had been for some time. In part, this reflected the administrative and other costs referred to above. In part, it reflected the customary tendency of these rates to remain unchanged for long periods of time and to lag behind changes in other types of interest rates.

State Interest Rate Ceilings

We said above that federal regulations on credit are intended to give the consumer fair treatment, but that the federal government doesn't set interest rates. Many states, however, *do* set ceilings on the interest rates that can be charged to consumers.

Spurred by pressure from lenders, there has been some tendency for states to eliminate interest rate ceilings and move toward deregulation, which several states have already done. Most states, however, continue to maintain some sort of ceiling on consumer credit. The majority have ceilings of from 18% to 21%. Some have ceilings below 18%, a few above 21%. And a few have "step" limitations—for example, a maximum of 21% on the first $750 of the outstanding balance, and a maximum of 18% on amounts over $750.

What the Stores Charge

Stores and banks have to respect the maximum rates set by each state in which they do business. However, where not limited by state rules, many stores currently charge an 18% to 21% APR on their revolving credit accounts. As we'll see in a moment, this is a bit higher than the average rate charged by banks. But to encourage customer loyalty and minimize dissatisfaction, stores usually impose very few additional charges. Ordinarily there's no annual fee, and usually none of the miscellaneous charges that some banks impose.

As a promotional tool, stores sometimes give you a deferred billing privilege that amounts to a free credit period—sometimes for special promotions, most familiarly at Christmastime. For example, you may be allowed to buy up to your credit limit from October through December and not be billed until January. If you pay the total amount when billed, there's no credit charge. Obviously, two or three months' free credit is a meaningful concession when you consider that the store's probable APR of 21% annually is equivalent to 1.75% per month.

What the Banks Charge

As we suggested in Chapter 3, bank charges on credit cards vary quite widely and, if the charges concern you, shopping around can produce some surprising differences.

The major banks generally charge annual fees of between $10 and $20 for Visa or MasterCard. Some banks offer a discount on the fees if you take both cards. And there are still a few banks that charge no annual fee at all.

As of early 1987, most banks were applying an APR of between 16% and 20% to Visa and MasterCard accounts. A few were lower, one or two higher. While this sounds cheaper than store credit, remember that the banks, unlike the stores, also impose an annual fee. While there's no way of making a strict comparison, consider that the average debit balance on bank credit cards is estimated to be around $700 per card. If bank credit in a particular case is 2% cheaper than store credit (say 19% against 21%), the 2% saved on an average balance of $700 amounts to $14 annually— probably just enough to offset the annual fee on the card.

So on an annual basis, the bank card may cost about the same as the store account. But of course there are other advantages to the bank card, which can be used widely rather than in only one store or chain; and once you have the bank card, using it rather than the store charge account may save you a few dollars. The fact that a store has its own charge account system ordinarily doesn't make it any less willing to accept bank cards, though of course the practice varies from place to place.

How the Banks Charge

The details of how you are charged on a bank card can vary widely, and you should give a careful reading to the bank's disclosure document before you sign up and pay the fee. Almost all banks charge interest on cash advances from the day of the advance, and give you a grace period on purchases of 25 or 30 days from the billing date. But be careful: there are a few banks that charge interest on purchases from the billing date or even from the purchase date. As we said earlier, you should avoid these unless there's some offsetting advantage.

Some banks impose a transaction fee on cash advances; some don't. A very few banks impose a transaction fee on purchases, which you should avoid. Obviously, you should be wary of a bank that offers you a low APR on your outstanding balance but makes up for it by imposing all sorts of miscellaneous charges.

How Banks Compute Finance Charges

Assuming that the bank gives you the normal grace period on purchases, you can avoid finance charges completely by paying each month's bill in full by the due date. But if you don't, the bank will compute the finance charge in one of three different ways.

Let's say that your billing date is the fifth of the month. Between May 5 and June 4 you made three purchases on your credit card totaling $250, for which you are billed on June 5. There's no previous unpaid balance. If you pay by the due date, June 30, there is no finance charge for the June 5–July 4 period. But what if you pay just half of the balance, or $125?

If your bank is a very kind, friendly bank, it may charge you on the "adjusted balance" basis. The adjusted balance is the opening balance ($250) less any payments made during the period ($125). So you would be charged only on $125. If the interest rate is, say 1½% per month (an APR of 18%), your charge for the month would be $125 × .015 or $1.88. This method gives you the lowest charge.

If your bank is less friendly, it may charge you on the "previous balance" method. This means simply taking the opening balance of $250 and giving you no credit for your subsequent payment (unless, of course, you have made full payment). In this case your charge for the month would be $250 × .015 = $3.75. This method gives you the highest charge.

Most banks, in fact, use neither of the above methods, but instead use the *average daily balance* method. This, reasonably enough, gives you credit for your payment based on the date when the bank receives it. Let's say that your payment of $125 was made on June 25. Disregarding any new purchases or advances, your outstanding balance was $250 for 20 days (June 6–25) and $125 for 10 days (June 26–July 5). The average daily balance would be calculated as follows:

$$20 \text{ days} \times \$250 = \$5,000$$
$$10 \text{ days} \times \$125 = \underline{\$1,250}$$
$$\text{Total} = \$6,250$$

Average daily balance = $6,250 divided by 30 days = $208.33
The finance charge under this method: $208.33 × .015 = $3.12.

Many banks impose other charges that you should be aware of. These vary not so much from bank to bank as from area to area, since the competitive situation in a given area is likely to govern what an individual bank will charge, and state regulations also may limit what the banks are permitted. California banks, for example, generally list a number of special charges.

Other Bank Charges

We've already mentioned the annual fee and the occasional transaction fee on advances. Some banks charge for a payment that arrives after the due date (or a certain number of days after the due date), and some impose a charge if you exceed your credit limit, even if you pay the balance promptly. There may be charges for an additional card, for replacement of a card, for photocopies of charge slips, or for bounced checks. Obviously, if you use your account carefully, most of these special charges can be avoided.

50

Pitfalls in Auto Financing

When you move into installment financing of big-ticket items, the unexpected costs can be more substantial. In the first place, auto financing is highly competitive, and marked by as much promotional selling as the Truth in Lending Act will allow. Keep your eye on the APR, and remember that a low interest rate is no bargain if it's offset by a higher price. Remember, also, that auto loans now often run for as long as five years, and that it's easy for a seller or lender to offer lower monthly payments by stretching out the payment period. To help you compare costs, here are some typical payment schedules on a $10,000 installment loan for three, four or five years:

Interest Rate	No. of Years		
	3	4	5
10%			
Monthly payment	$ 323	$ 254	$ 212
Total finance charge	1,616	2,174	2,749
12%			
Monthly payment	332	263	222
Total finance charge	1,957	2,640	3,347
14%			
Monthly payment	342	273	233
Total finance charge	2,304	3,117	3,961
16%			
Monthly payment	352	283	243
Total finance charge	2,657	3,603	4,591

Note: all figures are rounded to the nearest dollar.

Additional Auto Loan Costs

You need to be aware also of some of the less widely advertised elements in auto financing. Since the car is an expensive item, it's reasonable to expect that the lender will want to protect his or her loan by requiring you to take out collision insurance and other necessary insurance on your new car. But you have the right to choose where to arrange this insurance. If you are pressured or persuaded to arrange it through the lender, make sure that you're paying a competitive premium and are not giving a hidden bonus to the lender.

Credit Life Insurance

Another form of insurance that is often offered with auto loans, although technically it should not be required, is credit life insurance. This is a form of term life insurance, arranged so that if you die, the insurance will pay off the outstanding balance on your loan.

This may sound like a worthy and sensible idea, but the tie-in between the insurance and the loan often works to your disadvantage. First, in some cases the cost of the insurance is tacked onto your loan, so that you'll be paying finance charges on the premiums for the life of the loan. Second, the insurance is sometimes fixed at the total amount of the loan (say $10,000) for the full loan period, rather than being scaled down as the balance of the loan is paid off month by month. Finally, the premium rates may be higher than you could obtain on your own.

So, if you desire credit life insurance, try to arrange it yourself, and if possible shop several insurance companies in order to obtain the best premium rate.

Seeking the Tax Advantage

If you are planning to borrow in order to buy a car, a boat, or an expensive set of furniture, you are faced with the unpleasant fact that interest on such borrowings is "consumer interest," and the tax deduction for consumer interest is being phased out under the Tax Reform Act of 1986. (See Chapter 2.)

But there may be ways for you to borrow and still deduct the interest. One possible way out, if you are a homeowner, is to borrow against your home rather than against a car or boat. You can probably arrange for a second mortgage or a home equity credit line. (See Chapter 9.) If your total mortgage-type borrowings are no greater than the cost basis of your home, the interest payments will generally be tax-deductible; and the interest rate will probably be at least as low as, or lower than, the rates on most other types of borrowing. But the cost of arranging a second mortgage or home equity credit line may not be justified unless you intend to borrow a substantial amount, and for a fairly long period; and you should be aware of the other risks in this type of borrowing.

Another source of tax-deductible credit may be your investments. Interest paid on borrowings to buy or carry investments is still tax-deductible, within certain limits. (See Chapter 10.) If you borrow on your stocks or bonds to buy a boat or car, the interest will not be tax-deductible. But what if you were planning to pay cash for securities or other investments? You might consider reversing your plans, borrowing part of the cost of the investment (for example, you could buy securities on margin rather than putting up 100% cash), and using the cash you save for that boat or car. If you arrange the numbers carefully, you can end up with the same amount of debt, but in a form where the interest payments are tax-deductible rather than not.

PART V
YOUR CREDIT RATING

13·ARE YOU CREDITWORTHY?

In discussing types of credit and the costs of credit, we've talked as if you could get credit whenever you want it. Actually, in most cases you must *apply* for credit, and the lender must then decide whether you're a good credit risk—whether you are *creditworthy*.

Factors That Are Considered

What determines whether you are creditworthy or not? The lender first looks at your *ability to repay*. This means, first, looking at your income and job situation, and comparing them with your family obligations as well as your debts and any other financial obligations you may have.

The lender also looks at what you *own*—bank accounts, savings accounts, stocks and bonds, a home, or other property. Not only do these assets help ensure your ability to repay, they may be available to use as *collateral* which you pledge for the life of the loan to ensure repayment. Stocks and bonds, for example, are almost universally accepted as collateral and give you easy access to credit. Finally, the lender tries to judge your *reliability*, or *willingness to repay*. While this may sound like a subjective judgment, there are standard indications on which lenders rely. Have you repaid previous loans on time? Do you pay your rent, electric and phone bills on time? If you haven't been perfect, are there reasonable explanations? Can you offer good references? Do you have charge accounts that you've paid promptly? Is your bank account ever overdrawn? With this type of question, the lender tries to determine whether you're a good risk for this particular credit.

Many lenders use a "point scoring" system in an attempt to judge your creditworthiness systematically and impartially. While many factors may be taken into account, some of the items that might weigh in your favor (and give you positive points) are:

- A steady job (some lenders require that you have been at the same job for at least two years).
- Residence at the same address for a given time.
- Good references.
- A favorable long-term banking record.
- A favorable payment record on store credit and/or bank credit cards.

Some of the many possible considerations that might weigh against you and lower your point score are:

- Frequent job changes, or even a single job change in the last two years.
- A job in an unstable industry, or one where firings are frequent.
- Frequent changes of residence, or even a single change in the last two years.
- Too many debts outstanding.
- Lack of favorable references or cosigners.

The Equal Credit Opportunity Act

While a lender may legitimately turn you down on the basis of your record or financial position, the federal Equal Credit Opportunity Act *forbids* the lender to discriminate against you on grounds of *sex, race, color, religion, national origin,* or *marital status,* or because you are over a certain age. Also, a lender may not discriminate against you because you receive income from government sources such as welfare or Social Security.

If you're not creditworthy, don't expect the Equal Credit Opportunity Act to help you. But if you *are* creditworthy, it's an important protection. For example, consider a two-income couple applying for a home mortgage. The husband's income alone isn't enough to qualify them for the mortgage, but the two incomes together are more than adequate. Years ago, the lender might have taken the position that the wife was of child-bearing age and *might* leave her job to have children, and the mortgage might have been turned down on that basis. Now, since neither age, sex, nor marital status can be considered by the lender, the lender must give full consideration to the wife's income, and if the mortgage were rejected the couple could probably fight the rejection successfully.

14·THE CREDIT BUREAUS

Before discussing what to do if you're turned down for credit, let's examine where the lenders get the information they need in making credit judgments. Part of the information, of course, comes from your application. But lenders also rely heavily on a network of *credit bureaus* that compile and maintain information on tens of millions of Americans, including almost everyone who has used credit or even applied for it.

There are five major credit bureaus and a host of local ones, many of the smaller units being affiliated with one of the majors. Their files are built up and maintained by constant reports sent to them by most banks, stores and other organizations that grant credit.

If you've ever used credit, one or more of the credit bureaus in your area probably maintains a file with your name on it. It will contain information on your previous credit transactions and your payment record. It will list your address, birth date, Social Security number, and present employer (possibly with your position and income). Probably it will also include information about previous employers and residences and, if you're married, information about your spouse. And you can expect it to include information about any legal problems you have had, from lawsuits to bankruptcies.

Lending organizations supply information to the credit bureaus not only when credit is arranged, but usually every time you make a payment and on a regular monthly basis. So your file is completely updated to show your outstanding loan balances, any amounts past due, and any pattern of lateness. The file will also probably show all *inquiries* about you.

What about Your Right to Privacy?

Is all this information an invasion of your privacy? Not really. While it could obviously be subject to abuse, the law gives you considerable protection in that respect. Credit is, after all, a privilege rather than a right (though you do have the right to equal treatment). Creditors lose hundreds of millions of dollars every year because of delinquent borrowers; and the creditors, who are in a sense gambling on your creditworthiness, can hardly be blamed for trying to give themselves reasonable odds.

Protect Your Rating

It's obviously important for you to act so that your credit bureau file will make pleasant reading for prospective lenders. A little further on, we'll talk about some of the steps you can take to give yourself a favorable credit rating. First, to understand better how the credit bureaus work and what your rights are, let's discuss what you should do if you apply for credit and are rejected.

15·WHAT TO DO IF YOU'RE TURNED DOWN

The Procedure

Whenever you apply for credit, the Equal Credit Opportunity Act takes you under its wing. Under the Act, the lender must tell you within 30 days whether your application has been approved or not. If your application is turned down, the notice must be in writing, and it must either give you the specific reasons for your rejection or else tell you of your right to ask for those reasons. You must ask within 60 days, and if you want the answer in writing then your request must be in writing.

One possible reason for rejection might be that you have no credit history at all, and no file at the credit bureau. But if your rejection is because of information received through a credit bureau report, then another federal law, the Fair Credit Reporting Act of 1970, begins to work for you.

Fair Credit Reporting Act

Under this law, the lender must give you the name and address of the credit bureau that provided the adverse report, if that was the basis for your rejection. At this point, it's very important that you follow up and find out just what kind of information about you the credit bureau has in its file. Once you identify yourself adequately, a representative of the bureau must either show you the file itself or else discuss its contents with you and tell you most of the bureau's sources of information. In addition, the bureau must tell you who has received your credit report during the last six months.

What to Do about Wrong Information

If your file contains information that you think is wrong or inaccurate, you can demand that the credit bureau reinvestigate. If they find an error, or if they simply can't substantiate a piece of adverse information, they must correct the file and send a corrected report to anyone who has received your credit report in the latest six months.

Moreover, if after investigation the credit bureau decides to keep in its files an item with which you disagree, you can demand that the credit bureau place your version of the information in your file (limited to 100 words), send it to anyone who recently received a report on you, and also include it in future reports.

Charges for Investigations

Under the law, most of the above actions must be taken for you *without charge* if your credit application was denied because of information received from the credit bureau, and if you contact the credit bureau within 30 days after that.

Under other circumstances, there's likely to be a charge for making inquiry of a credit bureau. But it's important to note that you have the right at any time to contact a credit bureau and, for a reasonable fee (perhaps $15 or $25), to be told what is in your file.

Limitations on Credit File Contents

The law also puts limits on what the credit bureau can retain in its files. With certain exceptions, reports can't include adverse information that is more than seven years old, except that bankruptcy information can go back a full ten years. With enough patience, you can live down your past sins.

Note also that the credit bureau files include only information that relates to your finances, your credit record, and your creditworthiness. Contrary to what many people think, the files do *not* hold gossip about your morals, lifestyle, or other matters. If you have any doubts, ask to see your file.

Applicability

All the procedures we've described in case you're rejected for credit apply equally if a store or bank closes down your existing account. In either case, unless you know that the lender has good reasons for rejecting you, it's very important to follow up with the lender and, if necessary, the credit bureau.

Why Follow Up?

There are several good reasons why you should not let the matter drop. First, the lender or credit bureau may simply have made a mistake. Mix-ups between similar names are all too common, and you may have been saddled with someone else's information. Or, given the capacity for human error and post office error, a payment you made may not have been recorded properly.

Second, you may find that you've been rejected for a reason that turns out to be negotiable. Let's say you've just taken a new and better job and moved to a larger apartment. Under the point scoring systems that most lenders apply, these are likely to count as two negatives. But if you ask for an interview with a bank or store credit officer, there's a reasonable chance that you can convince him or her that you're a good credit risk.

Third, the simple fact that you follow up may show up as a plus on your credit record. The fact that *you* think you're creditworthy is important to a lender. If you seem to agree with the lender's judgment that you're probably not a good credit risk, you don't help your own case for the future.

Finally, if your rejection is based on solid reasons, it's better that you know what they are so that you can plan intelligently to put yourself in a better position for the future.

In any case, don't let a rejection discourage you from trying again elsewhere. Different lenders have different criteria, and you may qualify with one store or bank where you didn't with another.

And there's more you can do. In the next chapter, we'll discuss some of the steps you can take to improve your credit rating.

16·BUILDING YOUR CREDIT RATING

Obviously, in our credit society, your credit rating is one of the most valuable possessions you have, and one that should not be treated carelessly.

Overcoming a bad rating takes time, but it's worth the effort.

Lack of Credit Rating

A more common problem, especially among young people, is the lack of any credit rating at all. It's estimated that perhaps 25% to 30% of all the inquiries sent by lenders to credit bureaus are returned blank because the individual has no information on file at all.

It sounds like a Catch-22 problem—how do you get credit if you haven't got a credit rating, and how do you build up a credit rating if you can't get credit? But it's really not that difficult, and there are a series of specific steps you can take to build up a credit rating within a reasonable period of time.

Steps to Take

First, get in the habit of paying your bills on time.

Second, establish a bank savings/checking account or, if the bank fees don't make it too expensive, separate savings and checking accounts. Manage the account carefully so that your checks never bounce.

Third, if possible, open charge accounts at one or two local stores. If you have a reasonable job and are frank in discussing your lack of credit background, many stores will accommodate you. But don't open more than one or two such accounts at a time; you don't want to look as though you're planning to go on a spending spree.

Fourth, borrow a little money even if you don't need it. The cheapest way to do this is through a "passbook loan" on your bank savings account. Since the bank is lending money to you against your own savings balance, rates are generally low.

Yes, if you really needed the money it would be cheaper to withdraw it from the account and put it back in later, but that wouldn't be a credit transaction. This way your perfect repayment record will be reported to the credit bureau and you'll begin to acquire the favorable credit personality you're looking for. You could, instead, take out a direct personal loan from the bank (if the bank would grant it), but that would carry a higher interest rate.

Also, whenever you're next buying something that can be bought on installments, do it that way, even though you have the cash available, and even though the finance charges may add 10% or so to your total cash cost. (You will recoup part of this by letting your cash earn interest for you in a savings account or money market account while the installment loan is being paid off.) An appliance, a piece of furniture or a piece of jewelry all might be candidates for this type of purchase.

If you own a car or drive regularly, apply for a gasoline credit card.

If you're a college senior or recent graduate, and you're offered unsolicited charge accounts or credit cards, take them (within reason), even if you have no immediate need. The offer may not be repeated later on, and meanwhile you have a prime opportunity to build your credit rating. Even if you don't get unsolicited offers, you may find that the combination of your college degree and evidence of a good new job may win credit approval for you even if you fall short on other points.

After you have taken some of the above steps over a reasonable period of time, try applying for a Visa or MasterCard account. Try talking to officers at more than one bank to find out where your chances of approval are best.

Get References

If you're turned down on any of the above items, try to get someone reputable to act as a reference and possibly as a cosigner on one or more of your accounts. Also, before considering any of the formal procedures we discussed above in case of rejection, try to talk to someone at the bank or store where you are having problems, and see if you can convince them to start you off with credit on a small scale until you've had a chance to prove yourself. Your persistence will probably be respected, especially if you can show that your need for credit is legitimate and that you're not a spendthrift.

Some of the above steps may put you to a certain amount of expense. We think it's worth it. As we said above, a good credit rating can be one of the most valuable possessions you have. The cost of a small loan or installment purchase is probably a small price to pay for this valuable asset.

17·WOMEN AND CREDIT

As we noted above, the Equal Credit Opportunity Act forbids creditors to discriminate on the basis of sex or marital status. While this has been a big help, women—especially women who are or have been married—still often face special problems in establishing credit ratings and obtaining credit.

Why? There are several reasons. Under the Equal Credit Opportunity Act, as we noted, lenders can't discriminate based on sex or marital status. But they are still free to consider anyone's financial capacity and credit history. If a woman is a full-time homemaker with little property of her own, she may have trouble proving creditworthiness except to the extent a lender takes into account her husband's income and assets. Even if the wife has her own job, it's not uncommon that the family's major financial transactions are carried out under the husband's name alone.

The Equal Opportunity Credit Act

The Equal Credit Opportunity Act dates back only to 1975, a short time by historical standards. Its effects have not yet fully percolated through the economy, and many women don't know how to take advantage of its provisions.

What a Lender Can't Ask

The anti-discrimination clauses of the Act are clear. A creditor may *not* ask your sex on a credit application, except in the special case of a home mortgage; and in that special case, you don't have to answer.

You don't have to use a courtesy title (Ms., Miss or Mrs.) if you don't want to. If you're applying for an individual account, you can't be asked about your marital status unless the account will be secured by property in which your spouse has a legal interest, or unless you live in a community property state (Arizona, California, Idaho, Louisiana, Nevada, New Mexico, Texas and Washington). In cases where you *can* be asked about your marital status, the choice of answers must be limited to married, separated, or unmarried—with "unmarried" including single, divorced, or widowed.

You can be asked about the number of children you have, but you can't be asked about your *plans* to have children.

How the Law Helps Your Credit History

While these provisions are all to the good, you'll note that they don't help you directly to get a credit rating. But the law considers that problem also. A key provision requires that on all accounts used by both husband and wife, or on which both are liable, a creditor must report to the credit bureau in the names of *both* spouses, so that the credit bureau can maintain the history in the name of each spouse.

The law also says that where credit histories are used in rating your credit application, the creditor must consider the available history on any joint accounts as just described. And even where an account is only in the husband's name, a creditor is required to consider any information that the wife can offer to show that this history reflects her own credit history accurately.

What steps should a woman take to protect her own credit position?

If You Are Married

If you are married, make sure that all financial and credit accounts are carried under joint names except where there is good reason to keep them separate. This is particularly important for a full-time homemaker who otherwise may have no credit record.

Be consistent in your use of names. You can ask creditors and credit bureaus to carry your records under your maiden name (Beth Green) or your married name (Beth Finian) or a combination (Beth Green Finian or Beth Green-Finian) but *not* under your husband's name (Mrs. William Finian). Whatever you use, be consistent.

If You Are Getting Married

If you are getting married and intend to take on your husband's surname, carefully notify all creditors in writing and ask them to continue to maintain your credit file separately. As an extra precaution, check with the local credit bureaus a few months later and make sure that your records are being kept the way you've requested.

Joint Accounts

We've mentioned the requirement that credit transactions in joint accounts be reported to the credit bureaus in both names. But this rule dates back only to June 1977. If you have joint accounts that were opened *before* June 1977, notify each store, bank, etc., that you want the credit history reported to the credit bureau in both names. Then, after a few months, check with the credit bureaus and make sure that the information is being recorded properly in your own file.

Separate Credit Cards

Also, if you're a married woman, make every effort to have separate credit card accounts under your own name. It's worth the extra expense. Having a card with your name on it doesn't help your credit history if it's merely an extra card issued on your husband's account. If you're eventually widowed or divorced, having a favorable separate credit history will be more than worth any effort and expense that may have been involved.

If You're Recently Separated or Divorced

And one more note: if you've just separated or divorced, close down all joint accounts immediately unless there is some very special reason for not doing so. Presumably you're a good credit risk and don't want to be saddled with the possible delinquencies of your spouse or ex-spouse. If you find that your own credit standing has been impaired by the past delinquencies of your spouse, talk it over with your creditors and they will very possibly give you help in making a fresh start.

Are Women Better?

It's obvious that despite the Equal Credit Opportunity Act, women still face special problems in establishing credit ratings and obtaining credit. Some of the problems can be avoided by learning to make full use of the Act's provisions. Other problems are less easily solved. Credit is granted in large part on an individual's income, and it remains true that women's wages and salaries still often lag well behind those paid to men.

For a woman, persistence and face-to-face discussions with credit officers may help. Many credit officers—who, after all, are basically in the business of granting credit rather than refusing it—see the drive for women's equality as helping their own business. As one national credit executive told us: "Of course, we can't discriminate on the basis of sex. But if we could, we find that women are generally better credit risks than men."

PART VI
USING CREDIT WISELY

18·HOW MUCH CREDIT?

Once you've established your right to credit, how should you use it? Specifically, how *much* should you use it?

To the extent that you use charge accounts and credit cards rather than carrying cash, and have no trouble paying off your accounts in full each month before the due date, there's really no problem. You obviously have the money to cover these expenses, and are using credit only as a *convenience*, not as a financial resource.

When you use credit to buy goods and services for which you don't have the money available now, it's a different situation. Remember that credit doesn't add a penny to your income. It *does* permit you to buy things now that otherwise you would have to save for and buy later. Since you pay interest for this privilege, the use of credit becomes another expense.

Budget

If you expect to use credit in this way, it's important that you have a clear grasp of your financial position. Many people don't. Do you have a budget that shows where your income goes and how it's divided among various expenses? If you don't, now is a good time to begin.

There are several ways of setting up a budget, and you can do it in as much detail as you wish. At the simplest level, you should set down your monthly expenses in all categories, as fully as you can. The list of items might start off something like this:

- Rent (or mortgage)
- Electric and gas
- Telephone
- Food
- Household
- Meals out
- Entertainment
- Clothing
- Vacations
- Gasoline
- Auto insurance
- Life insurance
- Tuition
- Savings
- Etc.

It will probably take you a while to remember all the places your money goes in the course of a month or a year. You will almost certainly have to track your cash expenses carefully for at least a month, and perhaps for a few months, before you can complete the table accurately. Payments by check are of course easy to tabulate, and don't forget payments by credit card as well. In the case of checks and credit cards, you'll have to backtrack for 12 months to pick up the important items that you pay only once or twice a year. In the case of such occasional expenses as Christmas gifts, auto insurance, etc., take the annual total and divide by 12 in order to get a realistic picture of your monthly expenses over the whole year.

We've included the item "savings" under the list of expenses. Obviously, if your total other expenses are less than your income, the difference should equal savings, and you should have savings somewhere to show for it. If not, go back to the budget figures and see what has been left out.

Credit Planning

Once you have a grasp of the figures, you're ready to do your credit planning. If you're planning to buy anything on credit, from a TV set to a house, you will only be able to afford the monthly payments to the extent that:

1. You now have monthly savings.
2. You can reduce some other expenditures.
3. The purchase you're making will permit you to reduce other expenditures. For example, purchase of a car should eliminate your present expenses for car rentals. Purchase of a home will eliminate your present apartment rent.

With lifestyles and family situations varying so widely today, it's hard to state any general guidelines as to how much an individual or a family should borrow. Analysis of your own budget is the only reliable key. But it may be useful to look at some of the rules of thumb used by lenders and others.

Basic Borrowing Rules

Many mortgage lenders have traditionally used a "28/36" rule to judge what size mortgage a family could carry. The rule means that the monthly mortgage payments (principal and interest combined) should not be more than 28% of the family's gross monthly income; and total installment payments, including the mortgage, should not be more than 36% of gross monthly income.

Note the distinction between *gross monthly income*, which is salary before withholding taxes and other deductions, and *take-home pay*, which is the salary you actually receive after income taxes, Social Security taxes and other deductions are all taken out. Let's assume that these deductions take 20% of your gross income—that is, your take-home pay is 80% of your gross income. The 28/36 rule would then mean that mortgage payments could take up to 35% of your monthly take-home pay, and total debt payments could take up to 45%.

You'll note that the rule allows you to apply roughly 10% of your take-home pay to debt payments, excluding any mortgage. This is a relatively conservative figure; some people feel that 15% is still a manageable figure, and there are plenty of people who spend well over 15% of take-home pay on debt payments, particularly if they're paying off an automobile.

But we repeat that you have to think in terms of your own individual budget. You may choose to buy a large house, carry a large mortgage, and skimp on other items. Or you may be renting in a less expensive area and feel that you can afford more debt for other purchases. The percentages shouldn't necessarily bind you, but they should act as a useful warning. If you intend to exceed the guidelines, think twice (or three times) about your budget and whether your ability to repay is really sufficient to carry additional debt.

Credit Card Debt

Sometimes people make rational decisions about large commitments, but still let debt creep up on them in a hundred smaller ways. What size balances does it make sense to carry on charge accounts and credit cards? It's easy to let these revolving accounts get out of hand, especially in the case of the bank cards, where the minimum required payment may be as little as 3% or 4% of the outstanding balance.

You should worry seriously about your situation if:

- Your outstanding balances are steadily rising.
- You are only making the minimum required payments.
- Your balances are getting close to your credit limits.
- You are carrying a large number of charge accounts and/or credit cards, with outstanding balances on all or most of them.

You should also worry seriously if:

- You are taking cash advances to meet regular living expenses.
- You are delaying payment of month-end bills because your checking account is too low.

How to Avoid Trouble

In Chapter 24, we'll discuss what you should do if you have gotten so deeply in trouble that you can't find any way to meet your required debt payments. But if you are honest with yourself, the warning signals should save you before you get to that point. If any of the above descriptions applies to you, there are two steps you should take immediately:

First, stop using new credit. Bury your credit cards in a drawer and don't buy anything except what you can pay for by cash or check.

Second, go back to your budget and work on it until you have worked out a plan to reduce your total debt month by month. Obviously, this means that you will have to cut expenses somewhere. If you are married, the plan will only be successful if both spouses work it out together. Once you have made your plan, stick to it. While this is bound to be difficult, you should gain new inspiration as you actually see your total debt being reduced.

If you find that you are truly unable to reduce your debts and that your situation is, in effect, out of control, then you need professional counseling and help. Don't despair; take action immediately before the problem gets even worse. (See Chapter 24.)

19·THE ADVANTAGES OF USING CREDIT—WHEN TO BORROW

We live in a credit society. But many people are still suspicious of credit. Many older people, especially, grew up in a time when personal debt was frowned on, and when Shakespeare's "Neither a borrower nor a lender be" was considered sage advice. Is it really prudent to borrow?

When It's Good to Borrow

The answer, of course, is yes—if used carefully, borrowing can help your life. There are many circumstances in which the use of credit makes good sense. When credit gives you convenience without any interest cost—as when you charge an item at a store and pay in full before the due date—there's a clear benefit and no drawback. But in more substantial cases, you may borrow:

- To meet a genuine emergency, such as a medical crisis, a sudden need for major house repairs, etc.
- To help you make more money with which you can repay the loan—for example, to buy tools or clothes for a new job, or even a car.
- To buy something you need or very much want, where you have carefully decided that having the benefit sooner rather than later is worth the interest charges.
- To buy something on sale or at a bargain price, where you will pay a higher price if you wait. (But be sure the bargain is something you really need.)
- To buy something during a period of inflation,

when you are also sure that the price will be higher if you wait. (But remember that during periods of inflation, interest rates are likely to be high.)

- To buy a major asset, such as a house or car, which will last at least as long as the period over which you will repay the loan.
- To pay for college or postgraduate education, the benefits of which hopefully will last forever (or at least for life).
- To purchase earning assets that will create more wealth for you than the cost of the loan.
- To buy anything that you are convinced you are willing to sacrifice for sufficiently to pay off the principal and interest.
- To establish your credit rating and to prove your good character to the world. See Chapter 16 as to why this is one of the more important and valid reasons for borrowing. Remember that in the United States today, there are situations where all the cash in the world may not be as useful as a credit card.

Other Advantages of Credit

Credit carries other advantages that can make your life easier. It saves you from the trouble and possible danger of carrying large amounts of cash. It often lets you keep your cash more fully invested, since you know you have access to credit in case of sudden needs. It can give you peace of mind (a great asset) regarding possible emergencies. Renting automobiles and video cassettes becomes much easier. And credit accounts give you several minor benefits such as check-cashing privileges, access to special promotions, better treatment at stores, convenient telephone ordering, and a unified record of expenses.

The list of advantages is long. But for the other side of the story, see the next chapter.

20·THE DISADVANTAGES OF USING CREDIT—WHEN NOT TO BORROW

If we were all perfectly disciplined and controlled, there would be little to say on the disadvantages of credit. But credit is very easy to abuse; and when it is abused, the advantages quickly turn into disadvantages.

The Risk of Overborrowing

The biggest risk is that of becoming overextended—of borrowing more than you can repay. Remember what was said in Chapter 18 about budgeting. Credit doesn't give you brand new wealth. It simply lets you buy things sooner rather than later, assuming that you have carefully budgeted what you can repay. But too many people use credit to buy more than they can afford, and then have to find ways to meet interest payments as well.

The Temptation to Buy

Even if you're not overextended, credit often tempts you to buy things you don't really need. Later, when you are repaying the debt, you may well find that you can't afford things you really *do* need. In the enthusiasm of the moment, you may find that you have pledged more of your future income than you realized.

Also, credit isn't free. You pay interest (and often other charges) for the privilege of having something sooner rather than later. If you've calculated the cost carefully, you presumably know what you're doing. But many people don't realize what price they're paying for early gratification.

Be Wary of Easy Credit

In addition to the other warnings we have given you about the misuse of credit, you should be particularly wary of buying *anything* where easy credit is an important part of the promotion. Beware of the temptation to buy something you don't need, or to buy something you need sooner than you should buy it.

When the credit terms seem irresistibly good, make particularly sure that you are not signing up for "balloon" credit of some sort, where you make low payments for a while and must then suddenly pay the total balance in one lump sum. Don't gamble on your ability to come up with a lump sum in the future that you can't come up with today. While you may have high hopes of winning the lottery in the next year, remember the possibility that you might *not* win it.

Above all, draw up that budget we talked about as carefully as you can, and keep a copy close to you if you think you may be subject to temptation. And remember this quote from Charles Dickens:

> *Annual income twenty pounds, annual expenditure nineteen nineteen six, result happiness. Annual income twenty pounds, annual expenditure twenty pounds ought and six, result misery.*
> —*David Copperfield*

21·WHEN IS CREDIT A GOOD BUY?

In Chapter 12, we talked about the costs of credit, and pointed out how interest rates vary among different types of loans.

But how do you become a smart credit consumer? Is one type of credit necessarily good because it costs only 10%, and another type necessarily bad because it costs 21%? Are you being "ripped off" when you pay a higher rate?

Comparison Shop

The answer is that the credit field is highly competitive, and that competition in each field of lending tends to keep rates down to a level where lenders are not making an excessive profit. Individual lenders, of course, may try to take advantage of ignorant borrowers. But if you do your comparison shopping carefully, it's unlikely that any lender will be making a high profit from your loan.

Store Credit

If you carry retail store charge accounts, it's quite possible that the store is *losing* money on your account, despite the probable 21% APR (annual percentage rate). The cost of servicing these small accounts has climbed over the years, and the stores generally maintain them as a service to customers despite the lack of profitability.

If you tend to run a debit balance on your retail charge accounts and credit cards, you're paying for a relatively expensive service; the price you pay may be fair, but it isn't cheap.

The retail customer who comes off best is the one who uses the charge account or credit card regularly but pays in full before the due date. In this way you usually get between 25 and 55 days of completely free credit between purchase date and due date, plus the convenience of the charge arrangement. If you are this type of customer, you're making a profit off the system.

If you tend to carry regular debit balances in your accounts, your total finance charges over the long run may roughly equal the costs of the credit arrangements to your lenders. Then who is disadvantaged? It's most likely to be the cash customer, since the extra costs of the credit operation are built into the prices of all goods and services offered by a store, restaurant, or other establishment. The costs of credit may easily add 3% or more to prices. The cash customer pays this extra price and shares in none of the benefit.

Bank Cards

We pointed out in Chapter 12 that the average interest rate (APR) on bank credit cards is generally somewhat lower than on retail charge accounts. So once you've paid the annual fee, you may do a little better by using the bank card. But all these rates are high, reflecting the costs of servicing this type and size of account.

Big-ticket Items

As we've seen, in big-ticket loans such as car loans and home mortgages, rates are generally much lower, since the costs of servicing the loan are much smaller in relation to the size of the loan. But as pointed out in earlier chapters, there are differences not only in the rates on different types of loans, but in the tax-deductibility of the interest. One thing is certain: these other types of borrowings are almost always preferable to carrying large amounts of high-cost credit card debt.

22·BORROWING AND SAVING

At times in this book we've referred to the choice you often make between borrowing to buy something now, and saving to buy it later.

How do the numbers actually work out? Of course, the answer is different in every case. It depends on the interest rate you pay to borrow, the interest rate you could have earned on your savings, and the time period involved. Let's try an example.

Let's say that you are a music enthusiast and have decided to buy a new stereo set, complete with compact disk player and other attractions, for a price of $1,000. You have no extra cash available, but you've reviewed your budget and decided that you could afford payments of about $100 per month for a year.

The store would let you pay off the $1,000 in installments over a year at 21%, but balances on your Visa card are charged at an APR of 20%, you have a credit limit of $2,000, and you decide to do it that way. Ignoring the grace period, which doesn't change the comparison substantially, you can pay the debt off in 12 equal monthly payments of $92.64 each. Your total payments will be about $1,112, which means that the interest charges have added about $112 to the cost of your stereo.

Now let's say that you could have taken those 12 monthly payments of $92.64 each and invested them in a money market fund, or a bank money market deposit account, paying interest to you at the rate of 8%. At the end of the 12 months, you would have earned about $41 in interest, and your nest egg would have grown to $1,153—the $1,112 that it would have taken to buy the stereo on credit, plus the $41 in interest you have earned. If the stereo can still be bought for $1,000, it appears that you have saved $153.

Income taxes—which usually penalize you for saving, and sometimes reward you for borrowing—will reduce the savings advantage a little, but not much. If you decide to save rather than borrow, and you are in a 28% tax bracket, you will pay about $11 in tax to the IRS on the $41 of interest that you earn. Moreover, if you borrow, you may still be able to take a partial tax deduction for the interest you pay. (As we pointed out in Chapter 2, the deduction for this type of interest is being phased out over five years and will disappear in 1991.) All in all, your net saving-instead-of-borrowing benefit might be about $130 after taking taxes into account, rather than $153.

From there on the decision is up to you. Can you still buy the stereo for $1,000? If the price has gone up to $1,140, your saving is all eaten away, and you might as well have bought the stereo and enjoyed it a year earlier. If the price is still $1,000, would it have been worth the $130 to you to have had it a year earlier? You have to be the judge.

Obviously, you have to consider conditions as they are at the time. The 1986 tax law reduced the tax bite on savings, and made borrowing more expensive; but the tax laws could change again. As for inflation, the example above shows that when inflation is high and prices are rising, it may work out well to borrow—that is, to buy now and pay later. But remember that during high-inflation periods, interest rates also generally rise, which may cancel out the advantage of borrowing. Do the best calculation that you can, and consider each situation on its merits.

23·LOST CARDS, WRONG BILLS, AND OTHER PROBLEMS

With the tremendous volume of transactions that take place every day in revolving credit accounts, there's plenty of room for error. And errors do occur. Fortunately, there are laws which protect you, the credit consumer, from many of these errors—including your own.

Lost Credit Cards

Before we turn to the errors made by banks, stores, and computers, let's deal with the error *you* are most likely to make—loss of your credit card.

Of course, it may be theft rather than loss. But the procedures to follow are the same. First, you should keep a list of your credit card numbers somewhere separate from the cards. It's a good idea also to list the phone numbers to be called in case of emergency. But if you haven't kept such a list, or if you are away from it, you can get the same information from your latest bills. Phone each issuer *immediately* to report a lost or stolen card (and to begin the procedures for getting a replacement).

While you shouldn't delay, neither should you panic. You don't have to pay for any unauthorized charges made on your card after you notify the issuer of theft or loss. Moreover, the most you will have to pay for unauthorized charges made *before* you notify the issuer is $50 on each card. So your potential liability is not great.

Certain companies offer a service by which you list your credit cards with them and then, in case of theft or loss, make only a single call to them, and they make the calls to the individual card issuers. These services don't cost much, but our thought is—if you need this service, you're probably carrying too many cards.

Credit Card Billing Errors

Now, what about the errors that are inflicted on you by others? Most reputable banks and stores will make reasonable efforts to correct the kind of errors that inevitably occur on credit card and charge accounts. But if they don't, the federal Fair Credit Billing Act of 1975 gives you powerful protection to help you resolve disputes with creditors and to make sure that your accounts are handled fairly.

The Act applies specifically to open-end or revolving credit accounts. Among the kinds of billing error it covers are the following:

- Charges for items you never bought.
- Charges for items that were never delivered as agreed, or which you didn't accept on delivery.
- Charges that are incorrect in amount.
- Failure to record payments made by you.
- Failure to record items returned for credit.

In any of these cases, you should immediately phone the store or card issuer. If you don't get reasonably prompt satisfaction, you may want to be sure that you are protected under the Fair Credit Billing Act.

To get the protection of the Act, you must send a *separate written billing error notice* to the creditor. This notice must reach the creditor within 60 days after the mailing date of the first bill you received that contained the error. Send your letter to the address given on the bill for billing error notices. It's best to send it by certified mail, return receipt requested, so that you'll have proof of when your complaint was mailed and received.

Your letter must include:

1. Your name and account number.
2. A statement identifying the bill, stating that it contains an error, and giving the dollar amount of the error.

3. The reasons why you believe that the bill is mistaken.

If you want to send the bill and any other documents with your letter, *send photocopies only*. Keep the originals for your file.

Your complaint letter triggers several protective requirements. First, your complaint must be acknowledged by the creditor within 30 days after it has been received, unless the problem has been solved by then. Then, within two billing cycles (but not more than 90 days), the creditor must either correct the mistake or explain why the bill is thought to be correct.

While the dispute is going on, you may withhold payment of the disputed item, though you're required to pay all parts of the bill that are not in dispute.

Also, while the dispute is going on, the creditor can't take any legal action to collect the disputed amount, and your account can't be restricted in any way, except that the disputed amount may still be applied against your credit limit. And the creditor can't threaten your credit rating or report you as delinquent, though the creditor is permitted to report that you are disputing a bill.

Hopefully, the creditor's investigation will show that you are correct. In that case, the creditor must give you a statement of corrections and must remove all finance charges or other charges in connection with the erroneous item.

On the other hand, if the creditor still maintains that you owe part or all of the disputed amount, you must be notified in writing of how much and why. If this happens, and you still think you are right, you should write to the creditor within 10 days and say that you still refuse to pay the disputed amount.

However, at this point the protections of the Fair Credit Billing Act have run out on your case. Technically, you now owe the money (plus any finance charges); if you don't pay at least whatever minimum amount is now required, the creditor can start collection procedures, eventually even taking you to court.

Even now, though, all is not lost. There are several

last ditch efforts you can make—especially if you are sure that you are correct:

First, write to the president of the creditor organization. Presidents are sensitive about public relations, and sometimes this will get you a better response than you got from the credit department.

Second, write to your Federal Reserve Bank or to the Federal Trade Commission (FTC) and send a *copy* of the letter to the president of the creditor organization. The Federal Reserve System oversees consumer credit activities of banks, and the FTC oversees credit activities of stores and other nonbank organizations. The Reserve and the FTC don't directly represent individuals in particular disputes, but they may give you helpful information, and no creditor likes to think that he or she is under investigation by the government.

There are Federal Reserve Banks in Atlanta, Boston, Chicago, Cleveland, Dallas, Kansas City (Missouri), Minneapolis, Philadelphia, New York, Richmond, San Francisco, and St. Louis. You can write to the consumer affairs department of any of these, or you can write to the Director, Division of Consumer and Community Affairs, Board of Governors of the Federal Reserve System, Washington, DC 20551.

The FTC has regional offices in Atlanta, Boston, Chicago, Cleveland, Dallas, Denver, Los Angeles, New York, San Francisco, and Seattle. Or you can write to the Federal Trade Commission, Fair Credit Billing, Washington, DC 20580.

(Incidentally, both the Federal Reserve and the FTC publish many useful booklets on consumer credit and your various protections. It's worth writing for these even if you never expect to have a problem or dispute.)

Defective Merchandise

If you've bought goods or services on your credit card that you find to be defective in quality, the Fair Credit Billing Act has some help for you, even though this isn't strictly a billing error.

Under the Act, you can take the same legal actions

against the credit card issuer that you would be allowed to take under *state law* against the seller. Obviously, you have to find out your rights under state law, but usually you will have the right to withhold payment if you've been sold something defective.

First, you must try to resolve the problem directly with the seller. Then, if you made your purchase on a card issued by the seller, you can withhold payment. However, if you made your purchase on a bank card or another card *not* issued by the seller, you can withhold payment only if the purchase (a) was for more than $50 and (b) was made in your home state or within 100 miles of your home address.

Those Delinquent Deliveries

In case you hadn't noticed, the protective procedures discussed above give you an excellent way to handle the problem of deliveries of goods that don't arrive, or that don't arrive on time. When you expect to have something delivered, try whenever possible to pay with your credit card. If the goods aren't delivered, as sometimes happens, you simply exercise your right not to pay. Or if the delivery is too late to be useful—special party decorations that arrive on Tuesday, but the party was last Saturday—refuse delivery, and if you're charged anyway, refuse payment and if necessary explain to the card issuer what happened. It's much safer than paying and then trying to get a refund.

Peaceful Settlement

We hasten to add that most merchants and card issuers have no desire for disputes with their customers, and that you may well go through life without having to invoke the full protections of the Fair Credit Billing Act.

But the Act is important, and the fact that it is there puts added pressure on creditors to give you prompt, fair treatment. Know your rights, stand up for them, and you are likely to get better service and more respect.

24·WHAT TO DO IF YOU'RE IN TROUBLE

In Chapter 18, we suggested steps to take if you find your debts beginning to get out of control. But what if you're over the edge? What if your debts *are* out of control—if you can't meet the required payments, can't reduce the total you owe, and, in short, can't get out from under?

Be Up Front

Don't be afraid to talk to your creditors—at least, the ones you can't pay or have decided not to pay. If you have a legitimate temporary problem, they may be willing to work out revised payment schedules. For example, you may be the victim of a plant layoff, but you may have good reason to think that you'll be back at work in a month or two. Or you may have been fired, but have fair prospects of getting a new job soon. Or you may be the victim of a medical emergency. In such situations, creditors have nothing to gain by pushing you to the wall, and they will probably recognize that it's better to be paid slowly than not at all.

But what if you have no such excuse, but have simply and recklessly taken on more debt than you can pay off? We're assuming that you have taken the steps we recommended in Chapter 18—stopped incurring new debt, made every change you thought possible in your budget—and you're still in trouble.

Being Your Own Negotiator

If you think that you have the capacity to pay off your debts, but not at the rate your creditors expect, try talking to them. If you can show that you have a reasonable plan for digging yourself out, they may be willing to cooperate. They may even make some helpful suggestions as to how you can handle the problem.

Nonprofit Counseling Services

Probably, however, you need outside help. Fortunately, help for this kind of problem is quite easily available from a type of organization called a *consumer credit counseling service*. There are more than 200 of these nonprofit agencies around the U.S., and you can locate one by inquiring at your local United Way or other community organization. If that doesn't work, write to the National Foundation for Consumer Credit, 8701 Georgia Ave., Silver Spring, MD 20910, with which most of these local agencies are affiliated.

The counseling service may be able to help you solve your problem simply by budget counseling (usually free). If that isn't enough, they will help you work out a debt repayment program with your creditors; in this case there is likely to be a small charge for the service. The service may arrange for you to make one payment a month to them, from which they will pay your creditors. The arrangements can vary, but these nonprofit agencies generally have a fine record, and about 90% of the people who come to them for help are able to resolve their problems without bankruptcy.

Services to Avoid

There are also private very-much-for-profit organizations that offer to help you with debt repayment, consolidate your debts into one single-payment plan, perhaps arrange a new loan, etc. In most cases these organizations do very little for you, add an absolutely unjustifiable additional charge to your debt burden, and survive only because many people are ignorant of the existence of the nonprofit services described above. If you're in trouble, by all means avoid these and stick to the nonprofit organizations.

Also avoid the "credit clinics" that promise to clear up your record at the credit bureaus. For a sizable fee, these organizations will challenge the credit bureaus to substantiate all information they have on file regarding you. As we saw in Chapter 15, that's something you can do for yourself—and without paying the fee.

Avoiding Harassment

If you are seriously behind on your debt payments, it's quite possible that your life is being made at least slightly miserable by bill collectors. You may not know that the law limits the ways in which you can be harassed by independent debt collection agencies—that is, collectors other than the creditor organization itself. To learn your rights in this situation, contact the nearest regional office of the FTC (see Chapter 23) by mail or phone and ask for information regarding your rights under the Fair Debt Collection Practices Act of 1977.

Bankruptcy—The Last Resort

If all else fails, your debt problems may have to be settled in court. We probably don't need to tell you that bankruptcy is an extremely painful process which should be considered only as a last resort. You will need a lawyer, and the lawyer's fee and court costs will be added on to your other obligations.

Straight bankruptcy is resorted to when there is no practical possibility of an individual's paying all of his or her debts, even over a 10-year period. The person's assets are sold, except for a few protected items, and the proceeds are divided among the creditors, who typically get considerably less than they are owed. The balances owed are then canceled, but it is important to note that certain types of debt are *not* canceled. These include alimony, child support, most taxes, and most government education loans.

As an alternative, if the debtor can convince the court that he or she does have the ultimate ability to repay, the debtor may be placed under a different

92

procedure called the *Wage Earner Plan* (sometimes referred to as "Chapter XIII," from the section of the bankruptcy law from which it derives). Under such a plan, which generally must be approved by a majority of the creditors, the debtor makes regular prearranged payments to a court-appointed trustee, who in turn pays the creditors. The debtor must apply 20% to 30% of disposable income to the debt repayments, and must pay court costs as well as attorney's and trustee's fees.

So even in the late stages of debt sickness, there may be a way out. But the way out isn't easy. Better to watch for the early warning signs described in Chapter 18, and catch the disease in the early stages, when the only cure required is a small touch of self-discipline.

25·CONCLUSION

America is the land of credit. More than any other people, we buy goods and services on credit, and we borrow money freely when we need it.

Used well, credit can enhance your life and add to your pleasures and satisfactions. Yet few people really know how to use credit most effectively and economically. And while the cost of credit may be a significant part of your budget, few people shop for credit as carefully as they shop for a new car or even a new sweater.

The types of credit discussed in this book—credit cards, charge accounts, auto loans, cash borrowings, and other forms of credit—all take on meaning to the extent that they can make your life more convenient and more satisfying.

You owe it to yourself to become a better credit consumer. We will be pleased if this book has taken the mystery out of credit and helped you understand what credit is, when to use it, how to get it on the best terms—and, most important, how to use it carefully and wisely for your own satisfaction.

We wish you all success in the fine art of improving your life by making wise use of other people's money.

INDEX

ABOUT THE AUTHORS

ARNOLD CORRIGAN, noted financial expert, is the author of *How Your IRA Can Make You a Millionaire* and is a frequent guest on financial talk shows. A senior officer of a large New York investment advisory firm, he holds Bachelor's and Master's degrees in economics from Harvard and has written for *Barron's* and other financial publications.

PHYLLIS C. KAUFMAN, the originator of the *No Nonsense Guides*, is a Philadelphia attorney and theatrical producer. A graduate of Brandeis University, she was an editor of the law review at Temple University School of Law. She is listed in *Who's Who in American Law, Who's Who of American Women, Who's Who in Finance and Industry* and *Foremost Women of the Twentieth Century*.